THE COMPLETE COSORI ELECTRIC PRESSURE COOKER COOKBOOK

Linda Brown

All rights reserved. Copyright © 2018.

Contents

Introduction 3

Poultry 12

Pork & Beef 38

Fish & Seafood 64

Vegetables & Side Dishes 75

Vegan 86

Snacks & Appetizers 97

Desserts 108

INTRODUCTION

Do you want to make more home-cooked meals, quit spending money on takeouts, and eat better? Do you want to make time and energy to cook after a long busy day but you hate being organized? Then, you are in the right place! Home cooking has become a staple trend in the world.

There is no greater peace of mind than finding a great recipe and putting your favorite food into an electric pressure cooker, setting it, and relaxing with a glass of wine, knowing a perfectly made meal will be ready for you. We are talking about home-cooked meals and the Cosori Pressure Cooker, a health-oriented lifestyle that will make you a new person!

Whether you want to cook something quick and simple for a dinner or a special recipe for a holiday, you are sure to love your Cosori Pressure Cooker. This is a fast, convenient and easy way to make nutritious and great-tasting meals on a daily basis. In this cookbook, you will learn to cook almost everything in the Cosori Pressure Cooker, from fast and easy breakfast food to luxurious desserts and sophisticated casseroles. You are about to discover a beautiful world of pressure cooking that has changed millions of lives! Let's start our culinary journey!

Getting Started:
How to Use the Cosori Pressure Cooker

The world is facing global challenges – social and economic issues, environmental sustainability, global health, and so forth. We need new ways of doing things to open our minds to numerous possibilities! We need new ways to eat well and stay healthy for a lifetime. We need a super-sophisticated, multifunctional cookware such as the Cosori Pressure Cooker.

The Cosori Pressure Cooker is a unique, easy-to-use multi cooker that is designed to use higher temperatures and steam to cook food under pressure in a sealed chamber. High temperatures and pressure help your food to cook faster and healthier than conventional cooking methods. It uses a breakthrough technology to achieve perfect results that you just cannot replicate with any other cooking technique. The Cosori Pressure Cooker preserves vitamins and minerals while achieving great flavors and textures!

Recipes and cookware go hand in hand. The power of pressure cooking and Cosori Pressure Cooker is the power to combine ingredients, using an innovative formula to achieve the best culinary experience ever! In fact, you will have eight different appliances in your kitchen! You can cook big-batch recipes on Sunday and eat well during the week.

What can be cooked with the Cosori Pressure Cooker? You can cook any meat or vegetables in your Cosori Pressure Cooker; then, you can cook rice, grains, legumes, eggs, and so forth. Just make sure to consult a manual or recipe directions to set the timer.

How does it work in practice? Throw in a few common ingredients, press a preset button, and wait for the most delicious food ever. You can also customize your personal cooking programs. It really is as simple as that!

The Cosori Pressure Cooker is 8-in-1 multi-functional cooker so you can declutter your kitchen because you will not need additional cookware! This programmable multi cooker has eight built-in programs and an easy-to-read control panel that makes cooking easier than ever before!

"Delay Start" allows you to set your Cosori Pressure Cooker to start cooking later. You can also change cooking time, pressure or temperature by increasing and decreasing value; these functions offer lots of flexibility in the kitchen, creating a personalized cooking experience.

With so many preset buttons, you will become obsessed with your new Cosori Pressure Cooker.

Manual – this multi-function button allows you to come up with your own cooking programs. It has up to twelve hours of cook time and even six different pressure levels (Less/Low, Normal/Medium, More/High).

Poultry – this program is designed to cook all types of poultry meat. Chicken cooks all the way in about 10 to 20 minutes, 30 minutes for frozen. Turkey goes about 1 hour. It is impossible to overcook food in the Cosori Pressure Cooker; just try to use ingredients that have similar cooking times.

Soup – it is the fully automated function for cooking budget-friendly meals.

Meat/Stew – even the cheapest cuts of meat are made easy with this program. This cooking method is effective for roasts, ribs, and other pieces of meat that are typically braised for hours, but often they end up very dry and tasteless. If you are in a dilemma, meats like pork and beef absolutely cook all the way in about 40 minutes.

Slow Cook – this program is designed for everyone who wants a meal ready when they arrive home.

Steam Vegetables – an excellent choice for cooking and steaming delicate ingredients like vegetables.

Reheat – this is a useful function for everyone who loves leftovers because an extra day or two allows flavors to improve.

Yogurt – this function uses a two-step process: pasteurizing milk and culturing the yogurt.
Bake – this is the fully automated function for baking a bread, pudding and cake.

You can use your Cosori Pressure Cooker as a warming pot too. There are separate programs for white rice and brown rice so you don't have to worry about over-cooking and under-cooking. There is "Multigrain" setting that is perfect for quinoa, oatmeal and dumplings. "Steam Potatoes" is a fully automated function for cooking all types of potatoes.

Moreover, you can sauté vegetables and brown meat in your Cosori Pressure Cooker without an additional pans or pots. It is a good way to enhance flavors and aromas. By exploring healthy pressure cooker recipes and learning about your Cosori Pressure Cooker, you will be inspired to live an exceptional, healthy life. From now onwards, there's no excuse not to cook for yourself and your family!

Chef-Approved Tips for Better Pressure Cooking

The world's best chefs rely on pressure cooking, and now you can as well. Here are a few major points to remember:

If you want to cook meats and vegetables together, you should follow these simple steps: 1) Place your favorite vegetables on the bottom of the inner pot. 2) Rub the piece of meat with your favorite spice mix. 3) Place rack on top of vegetables for the best results (it will make it a little easier to remove the ingredients after pressure cooking but you can skip this step). 4) Lastly, pour in a liquid such as water, broth, cooking wine, beer, ale, or tomato sauce. Afterwards, you can separate ingredients if needed, and add them in two steps.

Certain food such as grains and legumes will expand during the cooking process, so do not fill the inner pot more than two-thirds full and don't pack the ingredients too tightly.

Food plating and presentation are just as important to the success of your dish as its taste; therefore, for better and appetizing presentation, always brown the meats before pressure cooking.

If you want to convert recipes from an old grandma's cookbook into pressure cooker recipes, you can do it by simply checking the cooking time for the individual ingredients. Keep in mind that the Cosori Pressure Cooker is ideal for beans, rice, grains, most meats and roast, as well as dense root veggies.

When it comes to dairy products, you can use them to make creamy and cheesy dishes in your Cosori Pressure Cooker. You should add them after the pressure cooking process is complete.

Finally yet importantly, feel free to experiment with these recipes and learn to create your own culinary masterpieces!

How You'll Benefit from the Cosori Pressure Cooker

There are many advantages of using the Cosori Pressure Cooker for making home-cooked meals.

1) Fast cooking

Fall off the bone ribs in under 25 minutes! Yes, it is possible! If you're like most of us, you have a tight schedule and don't have all day to spend in the kitchen. Setting an electric pressure cooker to cook your meal is an excellent solution, right? This is one of the greatest benefits of pressure cooking. These meals require little to no preparation and they can be made quickly, using only one cookware. These easy press-and-go functions will save you tons of time!

Bulk cooking is another key point because it can help you save time in the kitchen too. You can cook more serves of your favorite dishes and refrigerate leftovers for the next few days; you can also place your food in sealed containers and put them in the freezer; it's a great habit that can save you a lot of time.

And because your foods cannot overcook in strictly controlled environment, dinner is ready when you are! If you like precise, predictable results, you can simply rely on the Cosori Pressure Cooker. Using an electric pressure cooker in the kitchen is one of the smartest ways to make good food choices and find balance in life!

2) Nutrients are optimally retained in your food

We can all agree that home-cooked meals are much better and healthier than dining out. There is a long list of series diseases that are caused by junk foods. It includes diabetes, liver damage, stroke, obesity, high blood pressure, osteoporosis, and so forth.

Therefore, the essential nutrients are imperative for a healthy body. The key is to eat foods that provide a variety of nutrients! A home-cooked meal is an ideal solution for everyone who wants to eat healthier and look better. This is definitely of the most important benefits of electric pressure cookers – an ability to preserve vitamins and minerals. You can ensure your homemade version of favorite meal is free of additives and sugars!

Researchers have proven that cooking in a pressure cooker tends to keep vitamins and minerals better than other cooking methods. The Cosori Pressure Cooker has an airtight lid that locks into place; there's nowhere for vitamins to escape. A super-heated steam helps your food to retain its natural flavor and nutrition. Further, pressure cooking requires less oil and water. The last but not least, a shorter cooking time additionally helps preserve the nutrients in your food, awakening your palates to new tastes. The Cosori Pressure Cooker will jump-start your healthy lifestyle!

3) It saves money and energy

The Cosori Pressure Cooker really saves your time. The Cosori Pressure Cooker can brown meat, sauté onions and other vegetables, cook rice and porridge, bake cakes, boil pasta, steam potatoes and vegetables, and so forth.

In comparison to the conventional cooking methods, the Cosori Pressure Cooker is much less energy consumptive since it has a fully insulated housing. The Cosori Pressure Cooker is your lifesaver!

4) It is super convenient

Besides being a next-generation pressure cooker, it's also a rice cooker, steamer, slow cooker, sauté pan, warming pot, oven, and yogurt maker. With zero hands-on time, the Cosori Pressure Cooker offers you a peace of mind, because there is no steam, no smell, and no noise in your kitchen.

With your Cosori Pressure Cooker, you don't need to defrost food before pressure cooking; frozen food can go straight into the inner pot. Then, you can leave your device without supervision. You will end up with no cookware to clean afterwards, so say goodbye to dirty pots, burners and oven.

With your Cosori Pressure Cooker, breakfast becomes as easy as 1-2-3. It can be tempting to grab a donut or a bowl of cereal in the morning, but a fresh oatmeal can be ready in less than 5 minutes in the Cosori Pressure Cooker. When it comes to healthy lunch options, it's hard to beat the nutritional power of fresh vegetables. An awesome cooking setting named "Steam Vegetables" infuses flavor into fresh vegetables in no time! Moreover, there is a special setting named "Steam Potatoes" for your favorite root veggies. Further, you can have plenty of tender and juicy meats for your dinner. Your Cosori Pressure Cooker cooks the best dinners with high-quality, all-natural ingredients in record time. Fluffy potatoes or tender, braised cabbage sound much better than frozen meals for dinner.

There is an easy way to snack smarter. Throw veggie sticks into your Cosori Pressure Cooker and sprinkle your favorite homemade spice mix over everything. Add liquid ingredients such as honey, maple syrup, cooking wine, a broth, and so forth. Secure the lid and press the button. This is the easiest way to incorporate healthy fast snacks into your day and have more control over what is in them. In this way, low-fat and low-sugar mini-meals will not sabotage your dietary regimen! You can make impressive appetizers and sophisticated desserts such as lava molten cake or cheesecake right in your Cosori Pressure Cooker. The Cosori Pressure Cooker cuts down cook time so that you can easily plan family gatherings and dinner parties.

A Word about Our Recipe Collection

Most people think that cooking is time-consuming because many recipes require hours of preparation; in today's world, we simply don't have hours to spend in the kitchen. Pressure cookers utilize high temperatures to speed up the cooking time significantly. However, if you love good food and want to use the Cosori Pressure Cooker, this recipe collection might be for you. Forget difficult cooking methods, dried-out turkey roast, tough cuts of beef, and overcooked poultry. Meats can be perfectly juicy and vegetables amazingly crunchy! The most succulent fish in the world is pressure cooked too!

From traditional recipes that are passed down from generation to generation to new culinary innovations, we will explore 100 of the best pressure cooker recipes ever! Every recipe contains an approximate cooking time, the ingredient list, the number of servings, step-by-step directions, and nutritional information.

The Cosori Pressure Cooker is designed to provide pathways to transform your cooking experience and build a great, sustainable and bright future of eating and dieting. These recipes are a starting point; there are limitless ways to experiment with food in the Cosori Pressure Cooker, creating the kind of changes you want in your own kitchen.

However, the best way to experience the ins and outs of the Cosori Pressure Cooker is to try these recipes in your own kitchen. Learn to cook recipes for the next decade and bring the world's best dishes into your kitchen! Bon appétit!

POULTRY

1. Classic Chicken with Mushrooms and Red Wine 13
2. Mexican-Style Chicken with Cascabel Peppers 14
3. Ground Chicken with Tomato Sauce 15
4. Turkey, Zucchini and Cheese Casserole 16
5. Asian-Style Chicken with Mushrooms and Peanuts 17
6. Turkey Breasts in Sticky Apricot Sauce 18
7. Chicken with Fine Port Sauce 19
8. Greek-Style Chicken with Olives 20
9. Colorful Chicken Soup with Rose Wine 21
10. Festive Turkey Meatloaf 22
11. Grandma's Turkey Soup 23
12. Duck Breast with Mushrooms and Wine 24
13. Harvest Vegetables and Chicken Soup 25
14. Classic Creamy Chicken Salad 26
15. Hungarian-Style Stew (Paprikash) 27
16. Buffalo Chicken Wing Soup 28
17. Turkey and Cheese Meatballs 29
18. Winter Chicken Stew 30
19. Chicken Cutlets with Dry Sherry and Herbs 31
20. Chicken with Cheese-Parsley Dip 32
21. Italian-Style Cheesy Chicken 33
22. Chicken Fillets with Cheese and Peppers 34
23. Maple Roasted Turkey Thighs 35
24. Ground Turkey Chili with Beer 36
25. French-Style Chicken Wings 37

1. Classic Chicken with Mushrooms and Red Wine

(Ready in about 25 minutes | Servings 4)

INGREDIENTS

2 teaspoons peanut oil
2 chicken drumettes
1 chicken breast
2 shallots, chopped
2 cloves garlic, crushed
1/2 pound chestnut mushrooms, halved
1 cup vegetable stock
1/3 cup red wine

Sea salt and ground black pepper, to your liking
1/2 teaspoon red pepper flakes
1/4 teaspoon curry powder
1/4 cup tomato puree
2 teaspoons all-purpose flour
2 sprigs fresh thyme, leaves picked

DIRECTIONS

- Select the "Sauté/Brown" setting, adjust to "More/High", and press "On/Start". Now, heat the peanut oil and brown the chicken, skin-side down for 7 minutes or until browned; reserve.
- Then, add the shallots and sauté until they're tender and fragrant. Stir in the garlic and mushrooms, and cook until aromatic.
- Add 1/2 cup of vegetable stock and red wine, and scrape the bottom of your Cosori Pressure Cooker to loosen any stuck-on bits.
- Add the salt, black pepper, red pepper flakes, and curry powder; continue to cook, stirring constantly.
- Now, add the reserved chicken, tomato puree and the remaining 1/2 cup of vegetable stock. Sprinkle with all-purpose flour and fresh thyme leaves.
- Secure the lid. Choose the "Poultry" mode, adjust to "Normal/Medium", and press "On/Start"; cook for 15 minutes.
- Once cooking is complete, use a natural pressure release; carefully remove the lid. Bon appétit!

Per serving: 255 Calories; 12.1g Fat; 6.9g Carbs; 29.2g Protein; 2.7g Sugars

2. Mexican-Style Chicken with Cascabel Peppers

(Ready in about 15 minutes | Servings 3)

INGREDIENTS

6 chicken drumettes, skinless and boneless
Seasoned salt and ground black pepper, to taste
1/2 teaspoon red pepper flakes, crushed
1/2 teaspoon Mexican oregano
2 ripe tomatoes, chopped
2 garlic cloves, minced
1 teaspoon fresh ginger, grated
1 Cascabel chili pepper, minced
1/2 cup scallions, chopped
1 tablespoon fresh coriander, minced
1 tablespoon fresh lime juice
1 cup water

DIRECTIONS

- Press the "Sauté/Brown" mode, adjust to "More/High", and press "On/Start". Sear the chicken drumettes for 3 minutes on each side or until they are browned.
- In a bowl, mix the remaining Ingredients. Spoon the mixture over the browned chicken.
- Secure the lid. Choose the "Poultry" mode, adjust to "Less/Low", and press "On/Start"; cook for 8 minutes.
- Once cooking is complete, use a natural pressure release; carefully remove the lid. Bon appétit!

Per serving: 199 Calories; 4.3g Fat; 7.1g Carbs; 32.2g Protein; 3.4g Sugars

3. Ground Chicken with Tomato Sauce

(Ready in about 15 minutes | Servings 6)

INGREDIENTS

1 tablespoon olive oil
1 pound ground chicken
1/2 pound ground pork
2 garlic cloves, minced
1 yellow onion, chopped
2 tomatoes, chopped
1 cup chicken broth

Sea salt and ground black pepper, to taste
1/2 teaspoon paprika
1/2 teaspoon porcini powder
1/2 teaspoon fennel seeds
2 bay leaves

DIRECTIONS

- Select the "Sauté/Brown" mode and press "On/Start". Heat the olive oil and cook the ground meat until it is delicately browned; reserve.
- Sauté the garlic and onion in pan drippings for 2 to 3 minutes. Stir in the remaining Ingredients.
- Secure the lid. Choose the "Manual" mode, adjust to "Normal/Medium", and press "On/Start"; cook for 5 minutes.
- Once cooking is complete, use a natural pressure release; carefully remove the lid.
- Spoon the mixture on toasted slider buns and serve immediately.

Per serving: 329 Calories; 23.3g Fat; 3.2g Carbs; 25.1g Protein; 1.7g Sugars

4. Turkey, Zucchini and Cheese Casserole

(Ready in about 20 minutes | Servings 4)

INGREDIENTS

- 1 tablespoon sesame oil
- 1 pound ground turkey
- 1/2 cup Romano cheese, grated
- 1/4 cup breadcrumbs
- Salt and ground black pepper, to taste
- 1 teaspoon serrano pepper, minced
- 1 teaspoon garlic, smashed
- 1/2 teaspoon dried thyme
- 1 teaspoon dried basil
- 2 zucchini, thinly sliced
- 2 red bell pepper, sliced lengthwise into strips
- 1 cup tomato paste
- 1 teaspoon brown sugar
- 5 ounces Swiss cheese, freshly grated

DIRECTIONS

- Select the "Sauté/Brown" mode and press "On/Start". Now, heat the oil until sizzling.
- Then, sauté the ground turkey until it is delicately browned, crumbling it with a spoon. Stir in the cheese, crumbs, salt, black pepper, serrano pepper, garlic, thyme, and the basil.
- Cook for 1 to 2 minutes more; reserve.
- Wipe down the Cosori Pressure Cooker with a damp cloth; brush the inner pot with a nonstick cooking spray. Arrange 1/2 of zucchini slices on the bottom.
- Spread 1/3 of the meat mixture over the zucchini. Place the layer of bell peppers; add the ground meat mixture. Repeat the layering until you run out of Ingredients.
- Next, thoroughly combine tomato paste and sugar. Pour this tomato mixture over the layers.
- Secure the lid. Choose the "Manual" mode, adjust to "Normal/Medium", and press "On/Start"; cook for 10 minutes.
- Once cooking is complete, use a quick pressure release; carefully remove the lid.
- Afterwards, top your casserole with grated Swiss cheese; allow the Swiss cheese to melt in the residual heat. Bon appétit!

Per serving: 464 Calories; 24.4g Fat; 11.2g Carbs; 43.2g Protein; 1.8g Sugars

5. Asian-Style Chicken with Mushrooms and Peanuts

(Ready in about 30 minutes | Servings 4)

INGREDIENTS

1 pound chicken, cubed
1 teaspoon paprika
Salt and black pepper, to taste
1/2 teaspoon cassia
1 tablespoon butter, melted
1/2 cup honey
4 garlic cloves, minced

1 ¼ cups water
1/2 cup Worcestershire sauce
1/2 pound mushrooms, sliced
1 teaspoon Sriracha
1 ½ tablespoons lemongrass
1 ½ tablespoons arrowroot powder
1/4 cup peanuts, chopped

DIRECTIONS

- Select the "Sauté/Brown" mode, adjust to "More/High", and press "On/Start". Toss the chicken cubes with paprika, salt, black pepper, and cassia.
- Heat the butter and sauté the chicken for 4 minutes, stirring periodically. After that, stir in the honey, garlic, water, Worcestershire sauce, mushrooms, Sriracha, and the lemongrass; stir well to combine.
- Secure the lid. Choose the "Poultry" mode, adjust to "Normal/Medium", and press "On/Start"; cook for 15 minutes.
- Once cooking is complete, use a natural pressure release; carefully remove the lid.
- Select the "Sauté/Brown" mode and press "On/Start".
- To make the thickener, add arrowroot powder to a small bowl; add a cup or so of the hot cooking liquid and whisk until they're combined.
- Add the thickener to the Cosori Pressure Cooker and cook for 4 to 5 minutes more or until the sauce has thickened. Garnish with chopped peanuts. Bon appétit!

Per serving: 435 Calories; 12.3g Fat; 55.2g Carbs; 30g Protein; 41.9g Sugars

6. Turkey Breasts in Sticky Apricot Sauce

(Ready in about 30 minutes | Servings 8)

INGREDIENTS

2 teaspoons sesame oil
2 pounds turkey breasts, cubed
Sea salt and freshly ground black pepper, to taste
1 teaspoon red pepper flakes, crushed
1 teaspoon dried rosemary
1/2 teaspoon dried sage
1/3 cup Port wine
1/3 cup chicken stock, preferably homemade

For the Sauce:
1/3 cup all-natural apricot jam
1 ½ tablespoons rice vinegar
1 teaspoon fresh ginger root, minced
1/2 teaspoon chili powder
1/2 teaspoon soy sauce
3 teaspoons honey

DIRECTIONS

- Select the "Sauté/Brown" mode, adjust to "More/High", and press "On/Start". Now, heat the oil; sear turkey breasts, stirring occasionally, for 3 to 4 minutes.
- Season the turkey breasts with salt, black pepper, red pepper flakes, rosemary, and sage.
- Add Port wine and chicken stock to the Cosori Pressure Cooker and deglaze the bottom.
- Return the turkey to the Cosori Pressure Cooker and secure the lid.
- Choose the "Poultry" mode, adjust to "Normal/Medium", and press "On/Start"; cook for 15 minutes.
- Once cooking is complete, use a natural pressure release for 10 minutes; carefully remove the lid.
- Transfer the turkey breasts to a platter.
- Add the sauce Ingredients to the Cosori Pressure Cooker. Cook until the sauce reaches preferred consistency. Pour over the turkey and serve immediately. Bon appétit!

Per serving: 256 Calories; 10.2g Fat; 5.9g Carbs; 33.1g Protein; 5.2g Sugars

7. Chicken with Fine Port Sauce

(Ready in about 25 minutes | Servings 4)

INGREDIENTS

1 pound chicken legs, bone-in
1 cup tomato puree
1 cup vegetable broth
1/4 cup Port wine
2 shallots, cut into wedges
1 teaspoon fresh ginger, grated

2 cloves garlic, chopped
Salt and freshly ground black pepper, to taste
1 teaspoon dried oregano
1 teaspoon dried rosemary

DIRECTIONS

- Place the chicken legs in the Cosori Pressure Cooker. Pour in the tomato puree, vegetable broth, and Port wine.
- Choose the "Poultry" mode, adjust to "Normal/Medium", and press "On/Start"; cook for 15 minutes.
- Once cooking is complete, use a quick pressure release; carefully remove the lid.
- Stir in the remaining Ingredients.
- Secure the lid. Choose the "Manual" mode, adjust to "Normal/Medium", and press "On/Start"; cook for 3 minutes.
- Once cooking is complete, use a quick pressure release; carefully remove the lid. Serve warm and enjoy!

Per serving: 308 Calories; 17.6g Fat; 12.9g Carbs; 24.4g Protein; 6.2g Sugars

8. Greek-Style Chicken with Olives

(Ready in about 20 minutes | Servings 4)

INGREDIENTS

1 pound chicken drumsticks
1 cup chicken stock
1 cup tomato puree
1 rosemary sprig, chopped
2 thyme sprigs, chopped
2 garlic cloves, minced

Sea salt and ground black pepper, to taste
1/2 teaspoon smoked paprika
1 bay leaf
1/2 cup Kalamata olives, pitted and sliced

DIRECTIONS

- Add all the Ingredients to the Cosori Pressure Cooker; gently stir to combine well.
- Secure the lid. Choose the "Poultry" mode, adjust to "Normal/Medium", and press "On/Start"; cook for 15 minutes.
- Once cooking is complete, use a quick pressure release; carefully remove the lid.
- You can thicken the sauce on the "Sauté/ Brown" setting for a couple of minutes if desired.
- Divide the chicken drumsticks among serving plates. Top with the sauce and enjoy!

Per serving: 273 Calories; 14.4g Fat; 8.5g Carbs; 27.6g Protein; 3.6g Sugars

9. Colorful Chicken Soup with Rose Wine

(Ready in about 30 minutes | Servings 5)

INGREDIENTS

2 tablespoons olive oil
1 pound chicken drumettes
1 yellow onion, chopped
2 cloves garlic, minced
1 red bell peppers, seeded and sliced
1 green bell pepper, seeded and sliced
1 orange bell pepper, seeded and sliced
1 carrot, thinly sliced
1 parsnip, thinly sliced
1/4 cup Rose wine
Sea salt and ground black pepper, to your liking
1/2 teaspoon dried dill
1/2 teaspoon dried oregano
1 tablespoon granulated chicken bouillon
4 cups water

DIRECTIONS

- Select the "Sauté/Brown" mode, adjust to "More/High", and press "On/Start"; now, heat the oil until sizzling. Then, sauté the onion and garlic until tender and fragrant.
- Add the peppers, carrots and parsnip; cook an additional 3 minutes or until the vegetables are softened. Add a splash of rose wine to deglaze the bottom of your Cosori Pressure Cooker.
- Then, stir in the remaining Ingredients; stir to combine well.
- Secure the lid. Choose the "Soup" mode, adjust to "Normal/Medium", and press "On/Start"; cook for 25 minutes.
- Once cooking is complete, use a quick pressure release; carefully remove the lid.
- Remove the chicken wings from the cooking liquid; discard the bones and chop the meat.
- Add the chicken meat back to the Cosori Pressure Cooker, stir, and serve hot. Bon appétit!

Per serving: 238 Calories; 17g Fat; 5.4g Carbs; 16.4g Protein; 2.6g Sugars

10. Festive Turkey Meatloaf

(Ready in about 35 minutes | Servings 6)

INGREDIENTS

3/4 pound ground turkey
1/2 pound cooked beef sausage, crumbled
1/2 cup tortilla chips, crushed
1/2 cup dried bread flakes
1 tablespoon oyster sauce
2 eggs

1 onion, chopped
2 garlic cloves, chopped
Salt and ground black pepper, to taste
1 teaspoon cayenne pepper
1 cup tomato puree
3 teaspoons brown sugar

DIRECTIONS

- In a mixing bowl, thoroughly combine the ground turkey, beef sausage, tortilla chips, dried bread flakes, oyster sauce, eggs, onion, and garlic.
- Season with salt, black pepper, and cayenne pepper; stir until everything is well incorporated.
- Add 1 ½ cups of water and a rack to the bottom of your Cosori Pressure Cooker. Shape the meat mixture into a log that will fit onto the rack.
- Place the aluminum foil sling on the rack and carefully lower the meatloaf onto the foil. Mix the tomato puree with 3 teaspoons of brown sugar. Spread this mixture over the top of your meatloaf.
- Secure the lid. Choose the "Poultry" mode, adjust to "Normal/Medium", and press "On/Start"; cook for 30 minutes or to an internal temperature of 160 degrees F.
- Once cooking is complete, use a natural pressure release; carefully remove the lid. Bon appétit!

Per serving: 273 Calories; 14.8g Fat; 14.5g Carbs; 22.6g Protein; 4.5g Sugars

11. Grandma's Turkey Soup

(Ready in about 25 minutes | Servings 4)

INGREDIENTS

1 pound turkey breasts, boneless, skinless and diced

2 cups water

2 cups chicken stock

2 tablespoons apple cider vinegar

1 (28-ounce) can diced tomatoes

1 yellow onion, chopped

2 cloves garlic, minced

2 carrots, diced

1 teaspoon dried oregano

1/2 teaspoon dried marjoram

1/2 teaspoon dried thyme

1/2 teaspoon ground cumin

Salt and ground black pepper, to taste

12 ounces green beans, cut into halves

DIRECTIONS

- Place all of the above Ingredients, except for the green beans, into your Cosori Pressure Cooker.
- Secure the lid. Choose the "Poultry" mode, adjust to "Normal/Medium", and press "On/Start"; cook for 15 minutes.
- Once cooking is complete, use a quick pressure release; carefully remove the lid.
- Then, stir in the green beans. Seal the lid again; let it sit for 5 minutes to blanch the green beans. Bon appétit!

Per serving: 295 Calories; 12.2g Fat; 16.4g Carbs; 30.6g Protein; 8.4g Sugars

12. Duck Breast with Mushrooms and Wine

(Ready in about 30 minutes | Servings 4)

INGREDIENTS

1 pound duck breast, sliced
1/2 teaspoon red chili pepper
1 teaspoon cayenne pepper
1/2 teaspoon sea salt
1/2 teaspoon mustard powder
1/2 teaspoon freshly ground black pepper
1 tablespoon tallow, melted
1/4 cup Port wine
2 medium-sized shallots, sliced
2 garlic cloves, minced
1 (1-inch) piece fresh ginger, peeled and grated
1 pound wild mushrooms, sliced
1 cup water
1 mushroom soup cube

DIRECTIONS

- Season the duck breast with chili pepper, cayenne pepper, salt, mustard powder, and black pepper.
- Select the "Sauté/Brown" mode, adjust to "More/High", and press "On/Start". Then, melt the tallow. Sear the seasoned duck for 4 to 6 minutes, turning periodically; set it aside.
- Pour in the Port wine to scrape up any brown bits from the bottom of the Cosori Pressure Cooker. Stir in the remaining Ingredients.
- Secure the lid. Choose the "Manual" mode and press "On/Start"; cook for 20 minutes.
- Once cooking is complete, use a quick pressure release; carefully remove the lid. Serve immediately.

Per serving: 203 Calories; 8.5g Fat; 5.5g Carbs; 26.5g Protein; 2.7g Sugars

13. Harvest Vegetables and Chicken Soup

(Ready in about 20 minutes | Servings 6)

INGREDIENTS

1 pound chicken thighs
2 carrots, trimmed and chopped
2 parsnips, chopped
1 celery with leaves, chopped
1 leek, chopped
2 garlic cloves, minced
6 cups chicken stock, preferably homemade

1 teaspoon dried basil
1/2 teaspoon sea salt
Freshly ground black pepper, to taste
1 tablespoon fresh coriander leaves, chopped

DIRECTIONS

- Simply put all of the above Ingredients into your Cosori Pressure Cooker.
- Secure the lid. Choose the "Soup" mode, adjust to "Less/Low", and press "On/Start"; cook for 15 minutes.
- Once cooking is complete, use a quick pressure release; carefully remove the lid.
- Serve in individual bowls garnished with garlic croutons. Enjoy!

Per serving: 245 Calories; 14.6g Fat; 9.8g Carbs; 18.5g Protein; 2.7g Sugars

14. Classic Creamy Chicken Salad

(Ready in about 20 minutes + chilling time | Servings 6)

INGREDIENTS

1 ½ pounds chicken breasts
1 cup water
1 fresh or dried rosemary sprig
1 fresh or dried thyme sprig
2 garlic cloves
1/2 teaspoon seasoned salt
1/3 teaspoon black pepper, ground

2 bay leaves
1 teaspoon yellow mustard
1 cup mayonnaise
2 tablespoons sour cream
1 yellow onion, thinly sliced
1 carrot, grated
2 stalks celery, chopped

DIRECTIONS

- Place the chicken, water, rosemary, thyme, garlic, salt, black pepper, and bay leaves in the Cosori Pressure Cooker.
- Secure the lid. Choose the "Poultry" setting, adjust to "Normal/Medium", and press "On/Start"; cook for 15 minutes.
- Once cooking is complete, use a quick pressure release; carefully remove the lid.
- Remove the chicken breasts from the Cosori Pressure Cooker and allow them to cool.
- Slice the chicken breasts into strips; place the chicken in a salad bowl. Add the remaining Ingredients; stir to combine well. Serve well-chilled.

Per serving: 337 Calories; 23.7g Fat; 3.1g Carbs; 26.4g Protein; 0.9g Sugars

15. Hungarian-Style Stew (Paprikash)

(Ready in about 40 minutes | Servings 4)

INGREDIENTS

- 2 tablespoons butter, at room temperature
- 1 pound turkey legs
- Sea salt and ground black pepper, to taste
- 2 cups turkey stock
- 1/2 cup leeks, chopped
- 2 garlic cloves, minced
- 1 red bell pepper, chopped
- 1 green bell pepper, chopped
- 1 Serrano pepper, chopped
- 1 parsnip, chopped
- 1 cup turnip, chopped
- 1/2 pound carrots, chopped
- 2 tablespoons fresh cilantro leaves, chopped
- 1/2 teaspoon Hungarian paprika

DIRECTIONS

- Select the "Sauté/Brown" mode, adjust to "More/High", and press "On/Start"; melt the butter. Now, sear the turkey, skin side down, 3 minutes on each side.
- Sprinkle the turkey legs with salt and black pepper as you cook them.
- Stir the remaining Ingredients into the Cosori Pressure Cooker.
- Secure the lid. Choose the "Meat/Stew" mode, adjust to "Less/Low", and press "On/Start"; cook for 25 minutes.
- Once cooking is complete, use a natural pressure release for 10 minutes; carefully remove the lid.
- Transfer the turkey legs to a bowl and let them cool. Then, strip the meat off the bones, cut it into small pieces and return to the Cosori Pressure Cooker.
- Serve hot and enjoy!

Per serving: 403 Calories; 18.5g Fat; 17.1g Carbs; 40.9g Protein; 6g Sugars

16. Buffalo Chicken Wing Soup

(Ready in about 40 minutes | Servings 4)

INGREDIENTS

1 ½ tablespoons butter, softened
1 cup leeks, thinly sliced
Sea salt and freshly ground black pepper, to taste
1 pound chicken wings, halved
2 carrots, chopped
1 celery with leaves, chopped
2 garlic cloves, finely minced
3 cups water
1 tablespoon chicken granulated bouillon
1 tablespoon flaxseed meal
1 tablespoon champagne vinegar
1/2 cup garlic croutons, to garnish

DIRECTIONS

- Select the "Sauté/Brown" mode, adjust to "More/High", and press "On/Start". Now, melt the butter; sauté the leeks until just tender and fragrant.
- Now, add the salt, pepper, chicken, carrots, celery, and garlic. Continue to sauté until the chicken is no longer pink and the vegetables are softened.
- Add a splash of water to prevent burning and sticking. Add the remaining water and the chicken granulated bouillon.
- Secure the lid. Choose the "Soup" mode, adjust to "More/High", and press "On/Start"; cook for 35 minutes.
- Once cooking is complete, use a quick pressure release; carefully remove the lid.
- Select the "Sauté/Brown" mode and press "On/Start". Make the slurry by whisking the flaxseed meal with a few tablespoons of the cooking liquid.
- Return the slurry to the Cosori Pressure Cooker and stir to combine.
- Add the champagne vinegar and cook for 1 to 2 minutes more. Serve in individual bowls with garlic croutons. Bon appétit!

Per serving: 263 Calories; 9.9g Fat; 15.2g Carbs; 27.7g Protein; 3.3g Sugars

17. Turkey and Cheese Meatballs

(Ready in about 15 minutes | Servings 6)

INGREDIENTS

1 ½ pounds ground turkey
2 eggs
1 yellow onion, chopped
2 garlic cloves, minced
1 cup tortilla chips, crumbled
1/2 teaspoon paprika
Kosher salt, to taste
1/4 teaspoon freshly ground black pepper
1/2 teaspoon dried basil
1/2 teaspoon dried oregano
8 ounces Swiss cheese, cubed
1 tablespoon olive oil
1/2 cup tomato, pureed
1/2 cup water
1 tablespoon sugar
1/2 teaspoon chili powder

DIRECTIONS

- Thoroughly combine the ground turkey, eggs, onion, garlic, crumbled tortilla chips, paprika, salt, pepper, basil, and oregano.
- Roll the mixture into meatballs. Press 1 cheese cube into the center of each meatball, sealing it inside.
- Select the "Sauté/Brown" mode, adjust to "More/High", and press "On/Start"; now, heat the olive oil.
- Brown the meatballs for a couple of minutes, turning them periodically. Add the tomato sauce, water, sugar, and chili powder.
- Secure the lid. Choose the "Meat/Stew" mode and press "On/Start"; cook for 5 minutes. Once cooking is complete, use a quick pressure release; carefully remove the lid. Bon appétit!

Per serving: 404 Calories; 24.9g Fat; 9.6g Carbs; 35.3g Protein; 3.1g Sugars

18. Winter Chicken Stew

(Ready in about 20 minutes | Servings 4)

INGREDIENTS

1 tablespoon olive oil
1/2 cup shallots, chopped
2 carrots, trimmed and chopped
1 celery stalk, chopped
2 garlic cloves, minced
1/2 pound potatoes, peeled and quartered
2 ripe tomatoes, chopped
1 (15-ounce) can red kidney beans, rinsed and drained

1 cup chicken broth
1/2 cup dry white wine
1/2 cup water
4 chicken drumsticks
1/2 teaspoon salt
1/4 teaspoon ground black pepper
1 teaspoon cayenne pepper

DIRECTIONS

- Select the "Sauté/Brown" mode and press "On/Start". Then, heat the oil and cook the shallots, carrots, and celery until they are tender.
- Stir in the garlic; cook for another minute. Add the remaining Ingredients.
- Secure the lid. Choose the "Poultry" setting, adjust to "Normal/Medium", and press "On/Start"; cook for 15 minutes.
- Once cooking is complete, use a natural pressure release; carefully remove the lid.
- Then, pull the meat off the bones; return the chicken to the Cosori Pressure Cooker. Serve warm and enjoy!

Per serving: 463 Calories; 23.6g Fat; 19.8g Carbs; 41.1g Protein; 3.6g Sugars

19. Chicken Cutlets with Dry Sherry and Herbs

(Ready in about 20 minutes | Servings 4)

INGREDIENTS

1 pound chicken cutlets, pounded to 1/4-inch thickness
2 garlic cloves, peeled and halved
1/3 teaspoon salt
Ground black pepper and cayenne pepper, to taste
2 teaspoons sesame oil
3/4 cup water

1 ½ tablespoons dry sherry
1 chicken bouillon cube
2 tablespoons fresh lime juice
1 teaspoon dried thyme
1 teaspoon dried marjoram
1 teaspoon mustard powder
3 teaspoons butter, softened

DIRECTIONS

- Rub the chicken with the garlic halves; then, season with salt, black pepper, and cayenne pepper. Select the "Sauté/Brown" mode, adjust to "More/High", and press "On/Start".
- Once hot, heat the sesame oil and sauté the chicken cutlets for 5 minutes, turning once during cooking. Add the water and dry sherry and stir; scrape the bottom of the inner pot to deglaze.
- Secure the lid. Choose the "Manual" setting, adjust to "Normal/Medium", and press "On/Start"; cook for 5 minutes.
- Once cooking is complete, use a quick pressure release; carefully remove the lid.
- Reserve the chicken cutlets, keeping them warm.
- Stir the bouillon cube, lime juice, thyme, marjoram, and mustard powder into the cooking liquid.
- Select the "Sauté/Brown" mode and press "On/Start". Simmer for 6 minutes or until the cooking liquid has reduced and concentrated.
- Add the butter to the sauce, stir to combine, and adjust the seasonings. Pour the prepared sauce over the reserved chicken cutlets and serve warm. Bon appétit!

Per serving: 190 Calories; 8.4g Fat; 4.3g Carbs; 23.6g Protein; 2g Sugars

20. Chicken with Cheese-Parsley Dip

(Ready in about 1 hour 20 minutes | Servings 6)

INGREDIENTS

2 garlic cloves, minced
1 cup dry white wine
1 red chili pepper
Sea salt and ground black pepper, to taste
1/4 cup sesame oil
6 chicken drumsticks

Parsley Dip:
1/2 cup fresh parsley leaves, chopped
1/3 cup cream cheese
1/3 cup mayonnaise
1 garlic clove, minced
1/2 teaspoon cayenne pepper
1 tablespoon fresh lime juice

DIRECTIONS

- Place the garlic, wine, chili pepper, salt, black pepper, and the sesame oil in a ceramic container. Add the chicken drumsticks; let them marinate for 1 hour in your refrigerator.
- Add the chicken drumsticks, along with the marinate, to the Cosori Pressure Cooker.
- Secure the lid. Choose the "Poultry" setting, adjust to "Normal/Medium", and press "On/Start"; cook for 15 minutes.
- Once cooking is complete, use a quick pressure release; carefully remove the lid.
- In a mixing bowl, thoroughly combine the parsley, cream cheese mayonnaise, garlic, cayenne pepper, and the lime juice.
- Serve the chicken drumsticks with the parsley sauce on the side. Bon appétit!

Per serving: 468 Calories; 37.8g Fat; 2.1g Carbs; 28.7g Protein; 0.7g Sugars

21. Italian-Style Cheesy Chicken

(Ready in about 15 minutes | Servings 4)

INGREDIENTS

2 tablespoons butter, softened
3 garlic cloves, minced
2 rosemary sprigs, leaves picked
2 ripe tomatoes, chopped
1/2 teaspoon cumin, ground
1 teaspoon paprika

1/2 teaspoon curry powder
Salt and ground black pepper, to taste
4 chicken fillets, boneless and skinless
Water
1/2 cup 4-Cheese Italian, shredded
1/4 cup fresh chives, chopped

DIRECTIONS

- Select the "Sauté/Brown" mode, adjust to "Normal/Medium", and press "On/Start". Now, melt the butter.
- Add the garlic and rosemary, and sauté until they are fragrant.
- Now, stir in the chopped tomatoes, ground cumin, paprika, curry powder, salt, and black pepper. Top with the chicken fillets and pour in water to cover the chicken.
- Secure the lid. Choose the "Poultry" setting, adjust to "Less/Low", and press "On/Start"; cook for 8 minutes.
- Once cooking is complete, use a quick pressure release; carefully remove the lid.
- Select the "Sauté/Brown" mode, adjust to "Normal/Medium", and press "On/Start".
- Add the shredded cheese and cook 2 to 3 minutes more or until the cheese is melted. Serve right away garnished with fresh chopped chives. Bon appétit!

Per serving: 193 Calories; 12.5g Fat; 5g Carbs; 15.8g Protein; 2.3g Sugars

22. Chicken Fillets with Cheese and Peppers

(Ready in about 15 minutes | Servings 4)

INGREDIENTS

1 tablespoon olive oil
1 pound chicken fillets
2 cloves garlic, smashed
1 jalapeño pepper, seeded and chopped
1 white onion, chopped
1 red bell pepper, seeded and sliced
1 green bell pepper, seeded and sliced
1 orange bell pepper, seeded and sliced
1/2 teaspoon dried basil

1/2 teaspoon dried oregano
1 teaspoon dried sage
Kosher salt and ground black pepper, to taste
1 teaspoon cayenne pepper
1 cup roasted vegetable broth
1 cup heavy cream
1/2 cup cream cheese
1/2 cup Cheddar cheese, grated

DIRECTIONS

- Select the "Sauté/Brown" mode, adjust to "More/High", and press "On/Start". Now, heat the oil and cook the chicken for 2 to 3 minutes per side.
- Stir in the garlic, jalapeño pepper, onion, and peppers.
- Add the seasonings and gently stir to combine. Pour in the roasted vegetable broth.
- Secure the lid. Choose the "Poultry" setting, adjust to "Less/Low", and press "On/Start"; cook for 8 minutes.
- Once cooking is complete, use a natural pressure release; carefully remove the lid.
- Now, add the heavy cream, cream cheese and Cheddar cheese. Select the "Sauté/Brown" mode and press "On/Start".
- Cook until the cheese is melted and everything is thoroughly heated. Serve immediately and enjoy!

Per serving: 463 Calories; 32.3g Fat; 11.1g Carbs; 32.6g Protein; 6.1g Sugars

23. Maple Roasted Turkey Thighs

(Ready in about 30 minutes | Servings 6)

INGREDIENTS

2 tablespoons lard, melted
1 ½ pounds turkey thighs
Sea salt, to taste
1/2 teaspoon ground black pepper
1/2 teaspoon paprika

1 teaspoon dried dill weed
1 shallot, chopped
1 cup turkey bone broth
1 tablespoon maple syrup
1/2 cup dry white wine

DIRECTIONS

- Select the "Sauté/Brown" mode, adjust to "More/High", and press "On/Start"; melt the lard. Now, brown turkey thighs for 4 to 5 minutes on each side.
- Add the remaining Ingredients.
- Secure the lid. Choose the "Meat/Stew" setting, adjust to "Less/Low", and press "On/Start"; cook for 25 minutes.
- Once cooking is complete, use a natural pressure release; carefully remove the lid.
- Select the "Sauté/Brown" mode and press "On/Start" to thicken the cooking liquid. Spoon the sauce over the turkey thighs and serve warm.

Per serving: 257 Calories; 13.3g Fat; 5.6g Carbs; 27.2g Protein; 3.8g Sugars

24. Ground Turkey Chili with Beer

(Ready in about 25 minutes | Servings 4)

INGREDIENTS

1 tablespoon olive oil
2 garlic cloves, finely minced
1/2 cup shallots, finely chopped
1 carrot, sliced
1 bell pepper, chopped
1 jalapeño pepper, chopped
1 pound ground turkey
1 cup chicken bone broth

6 ounces beer
1 tablespoon cacao powder
1 tablespoon apple butter
1 teaspoon dried basil
1 (14-ounce) can tomatoes
1 (14-ounce) can kidney beans, drained and rinsed

DIRECTIONS

- Select the "Sauté/Brown" mode, adjust to "Normal/Medium", and press "On/Start". Then, heat the oil; cook the garlic, shallot, carrot, and bell peppers for about 5 minutes.
- Stir in the ground turkey and cook for 3 minutes more, crumbling with a fork. Add the remaining Ingredients.
- Secure the lid. Choose the "Poultry" setting, adjust to "Less/Low", and press "On/Start"; cook for 8 minutes.
- Once cooking is complete, use a quick pressure release; carefully remove the lid.
- Serve hot and enjoy!

Per serving: 484 Calories; 29.3g Fat; 14.1g Carbs; 41.5g Protein; 4.4g Sugars

25. French-Style Chicken Wings

(Ready in about 20 minutes | Servings 6)

INGREDIENTS

1 tablespoon butter, melted
2 pounds chicken wings, skin-on
2 garlic cloves, sliced
1 teaspoon mustard powder
1 teaspoon smoked paprika
Sea salt and ground black pepper, to taste
1/2 cup Pinot Grigio
1 cup tomato puree
1/2 cup water
1 cup cream cheese
1/2 lemon, cut into slices

DIRECTIONS

- Select the "Sauté/Brown" mode, adjust to "More/High", and press "On/Start". Melt the butter and brown the chicken wings for 1 to 2 minutes on each side.
- Stir in the garlic, mustard powder, paprika, salt, black pepper, Pinot Grigio, tomato puree, and water.
- Secure the lid. Choose the "Poultry" setting, adjust to "Normal/Medium", and press "On/Start"; cook for 15 minutes.
- Once cooking is complete, use a quick pressure release; carefully remove the lid.
- Serve with cream cheese and lemon slices. Bon appétit!

Per serving: 273 Calories; 14.1g Fat; 5.3g Carbs; 27.8g Protein; 2.9g Sugars

PORK & BEEF

26. Summer Pork Roast 39
27. Pork Shoulder with Riesling Sauce 40
28. Shoulder Roast with Potato
    and Peppers 41
29. Indian-Style Beef Curry 42
30. Chunky Ground Beef Soup 43
31. Juicy Beef Brisket with Cole Slaw 44
32. Pilaf with Ground Beef and
    Tomato 45
33. Osso Buco with Herbs and Wine 46
34. Balkan Pot Stew 47
35. Country-Style Chuck Roast 48
36. Steak with Wine Marinara Sauce 49
37. Next Level Mexican Tacos 50
38. Sticky and Spicy Spare Ribs 51
39. Rainbow Pork Chop Soup 52
40. Pork Taquitos with Manchego
    Cheese 53
41. Authentic Beef Goulash 54
42. Bacon, Beef and Cheese
    Sandwiches 55
43. Traditional Stroganoff with
    Rose Wine 56
44. Sticky Pulled Pork with Apples 57
45. Maiale Ubriaco (Drunken Pork) 58
46. Fancy and Spicy Pork Shoulder 59
47. Pork Soup with Tomato
    and Cheese 60
48. Western-Style Japanese Beef Stew 61
49. Ground Beef, Sausage and
    Cauliflower Casserole 62
50. Cajun-Style Back Ribs 63

26. Summer Pork Roast

(Ready in about 35 minutes | Servings 6)

INGREDIENTS

3 pounds pork butt roast
1/2 cup water
1 cup ketchup
1/4 cup champagne vinegar
3 tablespoons brown sugar

1/2 teaspoon sea salt
1/2 tablespoon fresh ground black pepper.
1 teaspoon ground mustard
1 teaspoon garlic powder

DIRECTIONS

- Add all of the above Ingredients to your Cosori Pressure Cooker.
- Secure the lid. Choose the "Meat/Stew" setting, adjust to "Normal/Medium", and press "On/Start"; cook for 30 minutes.
- Once cooking is complete, use a quick pressure release; carefully remove the lid.
- Shred the meat and return it back to the Cosori Pressure Cooker. Serve the pork roast with the sauce and enjoy!

Per serving: 435 Calories; 18.9g Fat; 15.1g Carbs; 48.8g Protein; 12.4g Sugars

27. Pork Shoulder with Riesling Sauce

(Ready in about 30 minutes | Servings 6)

INGREDIENTS

2 tablespoons lard, melted
2 pounds pork shoulder, cut into four pieces
2 garlic cloves, chopped
2 tablespoons honey
1/2 cup Riesling
1/2 cup water
1 tablespoon Worcestershire sauce
2 sprigs rosemary
1 sprig thyme
Kosher salt and ground black pepper, to taste

DIRECTIONS

- Select the "Sauté/Brown" mode, adjust to "More/High", and press "On/Start". Melt the lard. Then, sear the meat for 2 to 3 minutes, stirring frequently.
- Add the remaining Ingredients and gently stir to combine.
- Secure the lid. Choose the "Meat/Stew" setting and press "On/Start"; cook for 25 minutes.
- Once cooking is complete, use a quick pressure release; carefully remove the lid. Bon appétit!

Per serving: 483 Calories; 31g Fat; 7.3g Carbs; 38g Protein; 6.1g Sugars

28. Shoulder Roast with Potato and Peppers

(Ready in about 45 minutes | Servings 8)

INGREDIENTS

1 tablespoon tallow, at room temperature
3 pounds shoulder roast beef
1 teaspoon ginger garlic paste
Sea salt and ground black pepper, to taste
1 packet ranch dressing mix
1 ½ cups vegetable broth
4 pepperoncini peppers
2 pounds russet potatoes, peeled and quartered

DIRECTIONS

- Select the "Sauté/Brown" mode, adjust to "More/High", and press "On/Start". Now, melt the tallow. Sear the roast until it is delicately browned on all sides.
- Then, add the ginger garlic paste, salt, black pepper, ranch dressing mix, and vegetable broth. Top with the pepperoncini peppers.
- Secure the lid. Choose the "Meat/Stew" setting, adjust to "Normal/Medium", and press "On/Start"; cook for 30 minutes.
- Once cooking is complete, use a natural pressure release; carefully remove the lid.
- Shred the meat with two forks. Add the potatoes.
- Secure the lid. Choose the "Steam Potatoes" setting, adjust to "Less/Low", and press "On/Start"; cook for 10 minutes.
- Once cooking is complete, use a quick pressure release; carefully remove the lid.
- Serve the pulled beef with potatoes and enjoy!

Per serving: 313 Calories; 8.1g Fat; 24.8g Carbs; 34.6g Protein; 3.1g Sugars

29. Indian-Style Beef Curry

(Ready in about 15 minutes | Servings 6)

INGREDIENTS

1 tablespoon olive oil
2 pounds beef, ground
1/2 cup onion, chopped
2 cloves garlic, smashed
1 ripe tomato, diced
1 red chili pepper
Salt and ground black pepper, to taste
1/2 teaspoon ground cumin

1/2 teaspoon mustard seeds
1 teaspoon chili paste
1 teaspoon curry powder
1 cup water
1/2 cup light plain yogurt
2 tablespoons fresh green onions, chopped

DIRECTIONS

- Select the "Sauté/Brown" mode, adjust to "More/High", and press "On/Start". Heat the olive oil and cook the ground beef for 2 to 3 minutes.
- Then, process the onion, garlic, tomato and chili pepper in your blender. Add this mixture to the Cosori Pressure Cooker.
- Next, add the salt, black pepper, cumin, mustard seeds, chili paste, curry powder, and water.
- Secure the lid. Choose the "Manual" setting, adjust to "Normal/Medium", and press "On/Start"; cook for 5 minutes.
- Once cooking is complete, use a quick pressure release; carefully remove the lid.
- After that, fold in the yogurt and seal the lid. Let it sit in the residual heat until thoroughly heated. Serve garnished with fresh green onions. Bon appétit!

Per serving: 265 Calories; 12.5g Fat; 6g Carbs; 3.7g Protein; 4.4g Sugars

30. Chunky Ground Beef Soup

(Ready in about 30 minutes | Servings 4)

INGREDIENTS

1 tablespoon olive oil
1 pound ground beef
1 onion, peeled and finely chopped
Sea salt and ground black pepper, to taste
1 teaspoon cayenne pepper

1 parsnip, thinly sliced
2 carrots, thinly sliced
4 cups beef bone broth
2 garlic cloves, minced
1/2 cup tomato purée

DIRECTIONS

- Select the "Sauté/Brown" mode, adjust to "More/High", and press "On/Start". Heat the olive oil and brown the ground beef and onions until the meat is no longer pink.
- Add the remaining Ingredients to the Cosori Pressure Cooker.
- Secure the lid. Choose the "Soup" setting, adjust to "Normal/Medium", and press "On/Start"; cook for 25 minutes.
- Once cooking is complete, use a quick pressure release; carefully remove the lid. Ladle into individual bowls and serve hot. Bon appétit!

Per serving: 340 Calories; 16.3g Fat; 15.7g Carbs; 31.9g Protein; 7.2g Sugars

31. Juicy Beef Brisket with Cole Slaw

(Ready in about 1 hour 10 minutes | Servings 6)

INGREDIENTS

2 teaspoons olive oil
1 ½ pounds beef brisket
4 bacon slices, chopped
2 garlic cloves, pressed
1 carrot, chopped
1/2 cup dry red wine
1/2 cup water
2 sprigs rosemary
1/2 teaspoon mixed peppercorns, whole
1/4 cup tomato purée

1/2 teaspoon sea salt
1/2 teaspoon ground black pepper
1/2 teaspoon cayenne pepper

Cole Slaw:
1 head cabbage
1 yellow onion, thinly sliced
1 carrot, grated
4 tablespoons sour cream
4 tablespoons mayonnaise
Salt, to taste

DIRECTIONS

- Select the "Sauté/Brown" mode, adjust to "More/High", and press "On/Start". Then, heat the oil until sizzling. Sear the beef for 3 to 4 minutes or until it is delicately browned; reserve.
- Add the bacon to the Cosori Pressure Cooker; sear the bacon for approximately 3 minutes; reserve. Then, cook the garlic for 1 minute or until fragrant.
- Add the carrot, wine, water, rosemary, mixed peppercorns, tomato purée, salt, black pepper, and cayenne pepper. Return the beef brisket and bacon back to the Cosori Pressure Cooker.
- Secure the lid. Choose the "Manual" setting, adjust to "Normal/Medium", and press "On/Start"; cook for 60 minutes.
- Once cooking is complete, use a quick pressure release; carefully remove the lid.
- Meanwhile, make the cabbage slaw by mixing the remaining Ingredients. Serve and enjoy!

Per serving: 397 Calories; 29.4g Fat; 10.9g Carbs; 21.4g Protein; 5.1g Sugars

32. Pilaf with Ground Beef and Tomato

(Ready in about 15 minutes | Servings 4)

INGREDIENTS

1 tablespoon sesame oil
1/2 cup leeks, chopped
1 teaspoon garlic, minced
1 jalapeño pepper, minced
1 (1-inch) piece ginger root, peeled and grated
1 ½ pounds ground chuck
1 cup tomato purée
Sea salt, to taste
1/3 teaspoon ground black pepper, or more to taste
1 teaspoon red pepper flakes
2 cups Arborio rice
1 ½ cups roasted vegetable broth

DIRECTIONS

- Select the "Sauté/Brown" mode, adjust to "Normal/Medium", and press "On/Start". Now, heat the sesame oil and sauté the leeks until tender.
- Then, add the garlic, jalapeño, and ginger; cook for 1 minute more or until aromatic.
- Add the remaining Ingredients; stir well to combine.
- Secure the lid. Choose the "Manual" setting, adjust to "Normal/Medium", and press "On/Start"; cook for 7 minutes.
- Once cooking is complete, use a quick pressure release; carefully remove the lid. Serve immediately.

Per serving: 493 Calories; 28.8g Fat; 34.9g Carbs; 42.1g Protein; 3.3g Sugars

33. Osso Buco with Herbs and Wine

(Ready in about 30 minutes | Servings 8)

INGREDIENTS

2 tablespoons olive oil
1 ½ pounds Osso buco
2 carrots, sliced
1 celery with leaves, diced
1 cup beef bone broth
1/2 cup rose wine
2 garlic cloves, chopped

1 onion, chopped
2 bay leaves
1 sprig dried rosemary
1 teaspoon dried sage, crushed
1/2 teaspoon tarragon
Sea salt and ground black pepper, to taste

DIRECTIONS

- Select the "Sauté/Brown" mode, adjust to "More/High", and press "On/Start". Now, heat the olive oil. Sear the beef on all sides.
- Add the remaining Ingredients.
- Secure the lid. Choose the "Meat/Stew" setting, adjust to "Less/Low", and press "On/Start"; cook for 25 minutes.
- Once cooking is complete, use a natural pressure release; carefully remove the lid. Bon appétit!

Per serving: 302 Calories; 7.2g Fat; 21.7g Carbs; 34.3g Protein; 3g Sugars

34. Balkan Pot Stew

(Ready in about 40 minutes | Servings 6)

INGREDIENTS

1 tablespoon olive oil
2 pounds beef sirloin steak, cut into bite-sized chunks
1 cup red onion, chopped
2 garlic cloves, minced
1 pound bell peppers, seeded and sliced

1 cup vegetable broth
4 Italian plum tomatoes, crushed
Salt and ground black pepper, to taste
1 teaspoon paprika
1 egg, beaten

DIRECTIONS

- Select the "Sauté/Brown" mode, adjust to "More/High", and press "On/Start". Now, heat the oil. Cook the beef until it is no longer pink.
- Add the onion and cook an additional 2 minutes. Stir in the minced garlic, peppers, broth, tomatoes, salt, black pepper, and paprika.
- Secure the lid. Choose the "Soup" setting, adjust to "Normal/Medium", and press "On/Start"; cook for 25 minutes.
- Once cooking is complete, use a quick pressure release; carefully remove the lid.
- Afterwards, fold in the egg and stir well; seal the lid and let it sit in the residual heat for 8 to 10 minutes. Serve in individual bowls with mashed potatoes. Enjoy!

Per serving: 403 Calories; 21.3g Fat; 16.4g Carbs; 36.8g Protein; 8.7g Sugars

35. Country-Style Chuck Roast

(Ready in about 40 minutes | Servings 6)

INGREDIENTS

- 2 tablespoons lard, at room temperature
- 2 pounds chuck roast
- 4 carrots, sliced
- 1/2 cup leek, sliced
- 1 teaspoon garlic, minced
- 3 teaspoons fresh ginger root, thinly sliced
- Salt and pepper, to taste
- 1 ½ tablespoons fresh parsley leaves, roughly chopped
- 1 cup barbeque sauce
- 1/2 cup teriyaki sauce

DIRECTIONS

- Select the "Sauté/Brown" mode, adjust to "More/High", and press "On/Start". Now, melt the lard until hot.
- Sear the chuck roast until browned, about 6 minutes per side. Add the other Ingredients.
- Secure the lid. Choose the "Meat/Stew" setting, adjust to "Normal/Medium", and press "On/Start"; cook for 30 minutes or until the internal temperature of the chuck roast is at least 145 degrees F.
- Once cooking is complete, use a quick pressure release; carefully remove the lid.
- Serve with crusty bread and fresh salad of choice. Bon appétit!

Per serving: 252 Calories; 9.9g Fat; 9g Carbs; 30.1g Protein; 5.9g Sugars

36. Steak with Wine Marinara Sauce

(Ready in about 55 minutes | Servings 8)

INGREDIENTS

2 ½ pounds round steak, cut into 1-inch pieces
Kosher salt and freshly ground black pepper, to taste
1/2 teaspoon ground bay leaf
3 tablespoons chickpea flour
1/4 cup olive oil

2 shallots, chopped
2 cloves garlic, minced
1 cup red wine
1/4 cup marinara sauce
1/3 cup bone broth
1 celery with leaves, chopped

DIRECTIONS

- Toss the round steak with salt, pepper, ground bay leaf, and chickpea flour.
- Select the "Sauté/Brown" mode, adjust to "More/High", and press "On/Start". Once hot, heat the olive oil and cook the beef for 6 minutes, stirring periodically; reserve.
- Stir in the shallots and garlic and cook until they are tender and aromatic. Pour in the wine to deglaze the bottom of the inner pot. Continue to cook until the liquid has reduced by half.
- Add the other Ingredients and stir.
- Secure the lid. Choose the "Meat/Stew" setting, adjust to "More/High", and press "On/Start"; cook for 45 minutes.
- Once cooking is complete, use a natural pressure release; carefully remove the lid. Taste, adjust the seasonings and serve warm.

Per serving: 363 Calories; 17.9g Fat; 3.1g Carbs; 44.5g Protein; 1.1g Sugars

37. Next Level Mexican Tacos

(Ready in about 15 minutes | Servings 8)

INGREDIENTS

1 tablespoon olive oil
1/2 cup shallots, chopped
2 cloves garlic, pressed
2 pounds ground sirloin
1/2 teaspoon ground cumin
1/2 cup roasted vegetable broth
1/2 ketchup
Sea salt, to taste
1/2 teaspoon fresh ground pepper

1 teaspoon paprika
1 can (16-ounces) diced tomatoes, undrained
2 canned chipotle chili in adobo sauce, drained
12 whole-wheat flour tortillas, warmed
1 head romaine lettuce
1 cup sour cream

DIRECTIONS

- Select the "Sauté/Brown" mode, adjust to "Normal/Medium", and press "On/Start". Heat the oil and cook the shallots and garlic until aromatic.
- Now, add the ground sirloin and cook an additional 2 minutes or until it is no longer pink.
- Add the ground cumin, broth, ketchup, salt, black pepper, paprika, tomatoes, and chili in adobo sauce to your Cosori Pressure Cooker.
- Secure the lid. Choose the "Manual" setting, adjust to "More/High", and press "On/Start"; cook for 5 minutes.
- Once cooking is complete, use a natural pressure release; carefully remove the lid.
- Divide the beef mixture between the tortillas. Garnish with lettuce and sour cream and serve.

Per serving: 566 Calories; 33.4g Fat; 38.6g Carbs; 30.7g Protein; 6.5g Sugars

38. Sticky and Spicy Spare Ribs

(Ready in about 30 minutes + marinating time | Servings 6)

INGREDIENTS

1/4 cup honey
1/4 cup soy sauce
2 tablespoons hoisin sauce
1/4 cup tomato sauce
2 garlic cloves, smashed
1 teaspoon fresh ginger, finely grated
2 teaspoons sesame oil

6 country-style spare rib rashes
1 teaspoon chili powder
Salt and black pepper, to your liking
1/2 teaspoon ground allspice
1 teaspoon whole grain mustard
1 teaspoon smoked paprika

DIRECTIONS

- Thoroughly combine the honey, soy sauce, hoisin sauce, tomato sauce, garlic, ginger, and sesame oil in a bowl.
- Place the spare rib rashes in a large ceramic dish and pour over the honey/sauce. Cover with a plastic wrap and transfer to your refrigerator; let it sit at least 4 hours to develop the flavors.
- Add the spare rib rashes to the Cosori Pressure Cooker; add the remaining Ingredients, along with the reserved marinade.
- Secure the lid. Choose the "Meat/Stew" setting and press "On/Start"; cook for 25 minutes.
- Once cooking is complete, use a natural pressure release; carefully remove the lid.
- Now, press the "Sauté" button and continue to cook, uncovered, until the liquid is concentrated. Serve warm and enjoy!

Per serving: 388 Calories; 14.7g Fat; 19.2g Carbs; 42.2g Protein; 16.3g Sugars

39. Rainbow Pork Chop Soup

(Ready in about 35 minutes | Servings 4)

INGREDIENTS

2 tablespoons vegetable oil
3/4 pound bone-in pork chops
1/2 cup sweet onion, chopped
1 teaspoon fresh garlic, crushed
2 sweet peppers, deveined and chopped
4 potatoes, peeled and diced
2 carrots, trimmed and thinly sliced
1 parsnip, trimmed and thinly sliced
4 cups vegetable broth, preferably homemade

Salt and freshly ground black pepper, to taste
1/2 teaspoon paprika
1 teaspoon dried thyme
1 (1/2-inch) piece fresh ginger, grated
1 (1.41-ounce) package tamarind soup base

DIRECTIONS

- Select the "Sauté/Brown" mode, adjust to "Normal/Medium", and press "On/Start". Then, heat the vegetable oil and brown the pork chops for 4 minutes on each side.
- Secure the lid. Choose the "Soup" setting, adjust to "Normal/Medium", and press "On/Start"; cook for 25 minutes.
- Once cooking is complete, use a quick pressure release; carefully remove the lid. Serve hot with toasted bread. Bon appétit!

Per serving: 444 Calories; 16.9g Fat; 42.2g Carbs; 31.6g Protein; 5.1g Sugars

40. Pork Taquitos with Manchego Cheese

(Ready in about 1 hour | Servings 8)

INGREDIENTS

1 tablespoon lard, melted
2 pounds pork shoulder
1 tablespoon granulated sugar
1 teaspoon shallot powder
1 teaspoon granulated garlic
Salt and black pepper, to taste
1 teaspoon ground cumin
1 cup ketchup

1 cup tomato paste
1/2 cup dry red wine
1 teaspoon mixed peppercorns
2 bay leaves
1 teaspoon chipotle powder
1/2 cup Manchego cheese, shredded
16 corn tortillas, warmed

DIRECTIONS

- Select the "Sauté/Brown" mode, adjust to "More/High", and press "On/Start". Then, melt the lard. Sear the pork shoulder until it is delicately browned on all sides.
- Add the sugar, shallot powder, garlic, salt, black pepper, cumin, ketchup, tomato paste, wine, peppercorns, bay leaves, and chipotle powder.
- Secure the lid. Choose the "Meat/Stew" setting, adjust to "More/High", and press "On/Start"; cook for 45 minutes.
- Once cooking is complete, use a natural pressure release; carefully remove the lid.
- Shred the meat with two forks. Divide the shredded pork among the tortillas. Top with cheese. Roll each tortilla and brush it lightly with oil.
- Arrange the tortillas on a cookie sheet. Bake approximately 13 minutes and serve. Enjoy!

Per serving: 417 Calories; 24.4g Fat; 16.6g Carbs; 32.3g Protein; 11.8g Sugars

41. Authentic Beef Goulash

(Ready in about 35 minutes | Servings 4)

INGREDIENTS

1/3 cup all-purpose flour
Sea salt and freshly ground pepper, to taste
1 teaspoon garlic powder
1 ½ pounds boneless beef chuck, cut into cubes
2 tablespoons sesame oil
4 cups water

4 bullion cubes
1/4 cup rose wine
1 bay leaf
2 shallots, chopped
1 celery with leaves, chopped
2 carrots, sliced
1 red bell pepper, sliced
1 teaspoon Hungarian paprika

DIRECTIONS

- In a mixing bowl, thoroughly combine the flour, salt, black pepper, and garlic powder. Now add the beef cubes to the flour mixture; toss to coat well.
- Select the "Sauté/Brown" mode, adjust to "More/High", and press "On/Start". Heat the oil and sear the meat for 4 to 6 minutes.
- Add the remaining Ingredients and stir to combine.
- Secure the lid. Choose the "Soup" setting, adjust to "Normal/Medium", and press "On/Start"; cook for 25 minutes.
- Once cooking is complete, use a quick pressure release; carefully remove the lid.
- Serve in individual bowls and enjoy!

Per serving: 336 Calories; 16.6g Fat; 10.5g Carbs; 36.5g Protein; 1.2g Sugars

42. Bacon, Beef and Cheese Sandwiches

(Ready in about 1 hour 25 minutes | Servings 8)

INGREDIENTS

2 center-cut bacon slices, chopped
2 1/2 pounds top blade roast
Salt and ground black pepper, to taste
1 teaspoon dried marjoram
1/2 teaspoon dried rosemary
1 teaspoon Juniper berries

1 (12-ounce) bottle lager
1 ½ cups unsalted beef stock
8 slices Cheddar cheese
2 tablespoons Dijon mustard
8 burger buns

DIRECTIONS

- Select the "Sauté/Brown" mode, adjust to "More/High", and press "On/Start". Cook the bacon for 4 minutes or until crisp; reserve.
- Add the beef and sear for 8 minutes, turning to brown on all sides.
- In the meantime, mix the salt, pepper, marjoram, rosemary, Juniper berries, lager, and beef stock. Pour the mixture over the seared top blade roast.
- Secure the lid. Choose the "Manual" setting and press "On/Start"; cook for 1 hour 10 minutes.
- Once cooking is complete, use a quick pressure release; carefully remove the lid.
- Now, shred the meat and return to the cooking liquid; stir to soak well. Return the reserved bacon to the Cosori Pressure Cooker.
- Assemble the sandwiches with the meat/bacon mixture, cheddar cheese, mustard, and burger buns. Enjoy!

Per serving: 698 Calories; 40.1g Fat; 36.9g Carbs; 46g Protein; 19g Sugars

43. Traditional Stroganoff with Rose Wine

(Ready in about 35 minutes | Servings 6)

INGREDIENTS

2 tablespoons sesame oil
1/2 cup shallots, chopped
1 teaspoon minced garlic
1 bell pepper, seeded and chopped
1 ½ pounds stewing meat, cubed
1 celery with leaves, chopped
1 parsnip, chopped
1/2 cup rose wine

1 cup tomato paste
1/2 cup ketchup
1 can (10 ¾-ounce) condensed golden mushroom soup
9 ounces fresh button mushrooms, sliced
6 ounces cream cheese
1/4 cup fresh chives, coarsely chopped

DIRECTIONS

- Select the "Sauté/Brown" mode, adjust to "More/High", and press "On/Start". Heat the oil and sauté the shallots until they have softened.
- Stir in the garlic and pepper; continue to sauté until tender and fragrant.
- Add the meat, celery, parsnip, wine, tomato paste, ketchup, mushroom soup, and mushrooms.
- Secure the lid. Choose the "Meat/Stew" setting and press "On/Start"; cook for 30 minutes.
- Once cooking is complete, use a quick pressure release; carefully remove the lid.
- Stir the cream cheese into the beef mixture; seal the lid and let it sit until melted. Serve garnished with fresh chives. Enjoy!

Per serving: 536 Calories; 19.6g Fat; 45g Carbs; 50g Protein; 8.5g Sugars

44. Sticky Pulled Pork with Apples

(Ready in about 35 minutes | Servings 8)

INGREDIENTS

2 ½ pounds pork butt, cut into bite-sized cubes
1/2 cup vegetable broth
1/2 cup barbecue sauce
Sea salt and ground black pepper
1 teaspoon dried oregano
1/2 teaspoon dried basil
1 tablespoon maple syrup
1 red chili pepper, minced
1 cooking apple, cored and diced
1 lemon, sliced

DIRECTIONS

- Add the pork, broth, barbecue sauce, salt, black pepper, oregano, basil, maple syrup, chili pepper, and apple to your Cosori Pressure Cooker.
- Secure the lid. Choose the "Meat/Stew" setting and press "On/Start"; cook for 30 minutes.
- Once cooking is complete, use a natural pressure release; carefully remove the lid.
- Shred the pork with two forks. Return it back to the Cosori Pressure Cooker. Serve with lemon slices. Bon appétit!

Per serving: 434 Calories; 25.2g Fat; 13.6g Carbs; 36.1g Protein; 10.5g Sugars

45. Maiale Ubriaco (Drunken Pork)

(Ready in about 40 minutes | Servings 4)

INGREDIENTS

2 teaspoons olive oil
1 pound pork shanks, trimmed of skin
1 teaspoon turmeric powder
2 tablespoons vermouth
1 carrot, sliced
1 celery stalk, chopped
1 parsnip, sliced
1 bell pepper, deveined and sliced
1 serrano pepper, deveined and sliced
Sea salt and ground black pepper, to taste
1 teaspoon red pepper flakes, crushed
1 teaspoon garlic powder
1 cup beef bone broth
2 bay leaves

DIRECTIONS

- Select the "Sauté/Brown" mode, adjust to "More/High", and press "On/Start"; heat the olive oil. Once hot, cook the pork shanks until they are delicately browned.
- Stir in the remaining Ingredients.
- Secure the lid. Choose the "Meat/Stew" setting, adjust to "Normal/Medium", and press "On/Start"; cook for 30 minutes.
- Once cooking is complete, use a natural pressure release; carefully remove the lid.
- Serve warm over mashed potatoes and enjoy!

Per serving: 348 Calories; 25.1g Fat; 12.1g Carbs; 17.3g Protein; 4.5g Sugars

46. Fancy and Spicy Pork Shoulder

(Ready in about 55 minutes | Servings 6)

INGREDIENTS

1 tablespoon lard
2 pounds pork shoulder
1 cup broth, preferably homemade
1/3 cup honey
2 tablespoons champagne vinegar
1 teaspoon garlic, minced

2 tablespoons soy sauce
1 teaspoon aji panca powder
Kosher salt and ground black pepper, to your liking
1 tablespoon flaxseed, ground

DIRECTIONS

- Select the "Sauté/Brown" mode, adjust to "More/High", and press "On/Start"; melt the lard. Once hot, sear the pork shoulder on all sides until just browned.
- Add the broth, honey, vinegar, garlic, soy sauce, aji panca powder, salt, and pepper.
- Secure the lid. Choose the "Meat/Stew" setting, adjust to "More/High", and press "On/Start"; cook for 45 minutes.
- Once cooking is complete, use a natural pressure release; carefully remove the lid.
- Set the pork shoulder aside keeping it warm.
- Select the "Sauté/Brown" mode, adjust to "Normal/Medium", and press "On/Start". Add the ground flaxseed to the cooking liquid. Let it simmer until the sauce has thickened.
- Taste, adjust the seasoning and pour the sauce over the reserved pork shoulder. Bon appétit!

Per serving: 511 Calories; 30.7g Fat; 17.5g Carbs; 39.2g Protein; 16.4g Sugars

47. Pork Soup with Tomato and Cheese

(Ready in about 30 minutes | Servings 6)

INGREDIENTS

2 pounds pork stew meat, cubed
2 garlic cloves, smashed
1 teaspoon fresh ginger, grated
1/2 cup yellow onion, chopped
1 fresh poblano chile, minced
5 cups water
1 cup tomato paste

2 bouillon cubes
1 teaspoon dried oregano
1 teaspoon dried basil
Sea salt, to taste
1/4 teaspoon freshly ground pepper, or more to taste
1 cup Queso fresco cheese, crumbled

DIRECTIONS

- Place all of the above Ingredients, except for the Queso fresco cheese, in your Cosori Pressure Cooker.
- Secure the lid. Choose the "Meat/Stew" setting, adjust to "Normal/Medium", and press "On/Start"; cook for 25 minutes.
- Once cooking is complete, use a quick pressure release; carefully remove the lid.
- Divide the warm soup among serving bowls; top each serving with the crumbled cheese and serve immediately.

Per serving: 334 Calories; 10.6g Fat; 10g Carbs; 48.4g Protein; 6.1g Sugars

48. Western-Style Japanese Beef Stew

(Ready in about 30 minutes | Servings 6)

INGREDIENTS

1 tablespoon lard, at room temperature
1 ½ pounds ribeye steaks, cut into bite-sized pieces
1/2 cup shallots, chopped
4 cloves garlic, minced
Salt and black pepper, to taste
1/2 teaspoon sweet paprika
1 sprig dried thyme, crushed
1 sprig dried rosemary, crushed
1 carrot, chopped
1 celery stalk, chopped
1/4 cup tomato paste
2 cups beef bone broth
1/3 cup rice wine
1 tablespoon Tonkatsu sauce
1 cup brown rice

DIRECTIONS

- Select the "Sauté/Brown" mode, adjust to "More/High", and press "On/Start"; Now, heat the oil and cook the beef until it is delicately browned.
- Add the remaining Ingredients; stir to combine.
- Secure the lid. Choose the "Meat/Stew" setting, adjust to "Normal/Medium", and press "On/Start"; cook for 25 minutes.
- Once cooking is complete, use a natural pressure release; carefully remove the lid. Bon appétit!

Per serving: 368 Calories; 16.1g Fat; 30.9g Carbs; 25.5g Protein; 3g Sugars

49. Ground Beef, Sausage and Cauliflower Casserole

(Ready in about 35 minutes | Servings 4)

INGREDIENTS

1 head cauliflower, chopped into small florets
2 tablespoons olive oil
1/2 cup yellow onion, chopped
2 garlic cloves, minced
1/2 pound ground beef
2 spicy sausages, chopped
2 ripe tomatoes, chopped
1 ½ tablespoons brown sugar
2 tablespoons tamari sauce

Salt and freshly ground black pepper, to your liking
1 teaspoon cayenne pepper
1/2 teaspoon celery seeds
1/2 teaspoon fennel seeds
1 teaspoon dried basil
1/2 teaspoon dried oregano
1 cup vegetable broth
1 cup Pepper Jack cheese, shredded

DIRECTIONS

- Parboil the cauliflower in a lightly salted water for 3 to 5 minutes; remove the cauliflower from the water with a slotted spoon and drain.
- Select the "Sauté/Brown" mode, adjust to "Normal/Medium", and press "On/Start". Now, heat the oil and sweat the onions and garlic.
- Then, add the ground beef and the sausage and continue to cook for 4 minutes more or until they are browned.
- Stir in the remaining Ingredients, except for the shredded cheese, and cook for 4 minutes more or until heated through. Add the cauliflower florets on top.
- Secure the lid. Choose the "Manual" setting and press "On/Start"; cook for 8 minutes. Once cooking is complete, use a quick pressure release; carefully remove the lid.
- Top with the shredded cheese and let it melt for 5 to 6 minutes. Bon appétit!

Per serving: 523 Calories; 39.6g Fat; 10.9g Carbs; 30.8g Protein; 5.3g Sugars

50. Cajun-Style Back Ribs

(Ready in about 30 minutes | Servings 6)

INGREDIENTS

2 pounds baby back ribs
2 slices fresh ginger
1/2 cup dry wine
1 tablespoon brown sugar
2 cloves garlic, sliced

2 tablespoons soy sauce
1 cup beef bone broth
1 teaspoon Cajun seasoning
Sat, to taste

DIRECTIONS

- Add all of the above Ingredients to your Cosori Pressure Cooker.
- Secure the lid. Choose the "Meat/Stew" setting, adjust to "Less/Low", and press "On/Start"; cook for 25 minutes.
- Once cooking is complete, use a natural pressure release; carefully remove the lid. Serve warm and enjoy!

Per serving: 365 Calories; 25g Fat; 3.7g Carbs; 3.1g Protein; 2.6g Sugars

FISH & SEAFOOD

51. Coconut Fish Curry	65
52. Mahi-Mahi with Parmesan and Herbs	66
53. Piri Piri Fish Stew	67
54. Traditional Indian Masala Fish	68
55. Prawns with Halloumi Cheese and Olives	69
56. Clams with Bacon and White Wine	70
57. (South-Indian Curry) Meen Kulambu	71
58. The Perfect Tuna Salad	72
59. Home-Style Spanish Paella	73
60. Fresh Dill Shrimp Salad with Mayo	74

51. Coconut Fish Curry

(Ready in about 15 minutes | Servings 4)

INGREDIENTS

1 tablespoon olive oil
1 cup scallions, chopped
1/2 cup beef bone broth
1 pound halibut steaks, rinsed and cubed
1 cup tomato purée

1 jalapeño pepper, seeded and minced
1 teaspoon ginger garlic paste
1 tablespoon red curry paste
1/2 teaspoon ground cumin
1 cup coconut milk, unsweetened
Salt and ground black pepper, to taste

DIRECTIONS

- Select the "Sauté/Brown" mode, adjust to "Normal/Medium", and press "On/Start". Now, heat the olive oil; cook the scallions until tender and fragrant.
- Then, use the broth to deglaze the bottom of the inner pot. Stir in the remaining Ingredients.
- Secure the lid. Choose the "Manual" setting, adjust to "Less/Low", and press "On/Start"; cook for 7 minutes.
- Once cooking is complete, use a natural pressure release; carefully remove the lid.
- Taste, adjust the seasonings and serve right now.

Per serving: 325 Calories; 10.7g Fat; 17.2g Carbs; 38.6g Protein; 6.5g Sugars

52. Mahi-Mahi with Parmesan and Herbs

(Ready in about 15 minutes | Servings 4)

INGREDIENTS

2 ripe tomatoes, sliced
1 teaspoon dried rosemary
1 teaspoon dried marjoram
1/2 teaspoon dried thyme
4 mahi-mahi fillets
2 tablespoons butter, at room temperature
Sea salt and ground black pepper, to taste
8 ounces Parmesan cheese, freshly grated

DIRECTIONS

- Add 1 ½ cups of water and a rack to your Cosori Pressure Cooker.
- Spritz a casserole dish with a nonstick cooking spray. Arrange the slices of tomatoes on the bottom of the dish. Add the herbs.
- Place the mahi-mahi fillets on the top; drizzle the melted butter over the fish. Season it with salt and black pepper. Place the baking dish on the rack.
- Secure the lid. Choose the "Manual" setting, adjust to "Less/Low", and press "On/Start"; cook for 9 minutes.
- Once the cooking is complete, use a quick pressure release; carefully remove the lid.
- Top with parmesan and seal the lid again; allow the cheese to melt and serve.

Per serving: 376 Calories; 22.1g Fat; 9.4g Carbs; 34.2g Protein; 0.8g Sugars

53. Piri Piri Fish Stew

(Ready in about 15 minutes | Servings 4)

INGREDIENTS

- 1 pound fish, mixed pieces for fish soup, cut into bite-sized pieces
- 1 yellow onion, chopped
- 1 celery with leaves, chopped
- 2 carrots, chopped
- 2 cloves garlic, minced
- 1 green bell pepper, thinly sliced
- 2 tablespoons peanut oil
- 1 ½ cups seafood stock
- 1/3 cup dry vermouth
- 2 fresh tomatoes, puréed
- 1 tablespoon loosely packed saffron threads
- Sea salt and ground black pepper, to taste
- 1 teaspoon Piri Piri
- 2 bay leaves
- 1/4 cup fresh cilantro, roughly chopped
- 1/2 lemon, sliced

DIRECTIONS

- Simply put all of the above Ingredients, except for the cilantro and lemon, into your Cosori Pressure Cooker.
- Secure the lid. Choose the "Manual" setting, adjust to "Less/Low", and press "On/Start"; cook for 8 minutes.
- Once cooking is complete, use a quick pressure release; carefully remove the lid.
- Ladle the stew into individual bowls; serve with fresh cilantro and lemon. Enjoy!

Per serving: 342 Calories; 20.8g Fat; 14.7g Carbs; 24.6g Protein; 9.2g Sugars

54. Traditional Indian Masala Fish

(Ready in about 15 minutes | Servings 4)

INGREDIENTS

2 tablespoons olive oil
1/2 cup scallions, chopped
2 garlic cloves, minced
1/4 cup tikka masala curry paste
1/3 teaspoon ground allspice
1 (14-ounce) can diced tomatoes
1 tablespoon brown sugar

1 teaspoon hot paprika
1 cup vegetable broth
1 ½ pounds haddock fillets, cut into bite-sized chunks
1 cup natural yogurt
1 lime, cut into wedges

DIRECTIONS

- Select the "Sauté/Brown" mode, adjust to "Normal/Medium", and press "On/Start"; heat the oil. Then, sauté the scallions until tender and translucent.
- Now, add the garlic; continue to sauté for a further 30 seconds.
- Stir the curry paste, allspice, tomatoes, sugar, paprika, broth, and haddock into the Cosori Pressure Cooker.
- Secure the lid. Choose the "Manual" setting, adjust to "Less/Low", and press "On/Start"; cook for 5 minutes.
- Once cooking is complete, use a quick pressure release; carefully remove the lid.
- Then, fold in the natural yogurt and stir to combine well; seal the lid again and allow it to sit in the residual heat until warmed through.
- Serve in individual bowls, garnished with lime wedges. Enjoy!

Per serving: 273 Calories; 9.3g Fat; 13.5g Carbs; 34.9g Protein; 6.6g Sugars

55. Prawns with Halloumi Cheese and Olives

(Ready in about 10 minutes | Servings 4)

INGREDIENTS

1 tablespoon olive oil

1/2 cup scallions, chopped

2 garlic cloves, minced

Sea salt and ground black pepper, to taste

1/2 teaspoon cayenne pepper, or more taste

1 teaspoon dried oregano

2 ripe tomatoes, chopped

1 ½ pounds prawns, cleaned

6 ounces Halloumi cheese, sliced

1/2 cup Kalamata olives, pitted and sliced

2 tablespoons fresh cilantro, chopped

DIRECTIONS

- Select the "Sauté/Brown" mode, adjust to "Normal/Medium", and press "On/Start". Then, heat the oil; sauté the scallions and garlic until tender and fragrant.
- Add the salt, black pepper, cayenne pepper, oregano, tomatoes, and prawns.
- Secure the lid. Choose the "Manual" setting, adjust to "Less/Low", and press "On/Start"; cook for 3 minutes.
- Once cooking is complete, use a quick pressure release; carefully remove the lid.
- Ladle into serving bowls; top each serving with cheese, olives and fresh cilantro. Bon appétit!

Per serving: 351 Calories; 16.6g Fat; 11.9g Carbs; 37.8g Protein; 5.6g Sugars

56. Clams with Bacon and White Wine

(Ready in about 10 minutes | Servings 5)

INGREDIENTS

1/2 cup bacon, smoked and cubed
2 onions, chopped
3 garlic cloves, minced
1 sprig thyme
3 (6.5-ounce) cans clams, chopped
1/3 cup tarty white wine
1/3 cup water

1/2 cup clam juice
A pinch of cayenne pepper
1 bay leaf
5 lime juice
2 tablespoons fresh chives, roughly chopped

DIRECTIONS

- Select the "Sauté/Brown" mode, adjust to "Normal/Medium", and press "On/Start". Add the cubed bacon. Once the bacon releases its fat, add the onions, garlic, and thyme.
- Cook for 3 minutes more or until the onion is transparent.
- Add the clams, white wine, water, clam juice, cayenne pepper, and bay leaf.
- Secure the lid. Choose the "Manual" setting, adjust to "Less/Low", and press "On/Start"; cook for 4 minutes.
- Once cooking is complete, use a natural pressure release; carefully remove the lid.
- Ladle into individual bowls and serve garnished with lime slices and fresh chives. Bon appétit!

Per serving: 157 Calories; 4.6g Fat; 27.7g Carbs; 3.4g Protein; 8.3g Sugars

57. (South-Indian Curry) Meen Kulambu

(Ready in about 15 minutes | Servings 6)

INGREDIENTS

1 tablespoon olive oil
1 cup scallions, chopped
1 teaspoon fresh garlic, smashed
2 pounds mackerel fillets, cut into bite-size chunks
1 ½ cups coconut milk
1 cup chicken bone broth, preferably homemade

2 dried red chilies, coarsely chopped
1 teaspoon curry powder
1 teaspoon ground coriander
1 teaspoon cayenne pepper
Sea salt and ground black pepper, to taste
2 tablespoons freshly squeezed lemon juice

DIRECTIONS

- Select the "Sauté/Brown" mode, adjust to "Normal/Medium", and press "On/Start". Heat the oil until sizzling; once hot, sauté the scallions and garlic until tender and fragrant.
- Add the remaining Ingredients, except for the lemon juice, to the Cosori Pressure Cooker.
- Secure the lid. Choose the "Manual" setting, adjust to "Less/Low", and press "On/Start"; cook for 6 minutes.
- Once cooking is complete, use a quick pressure release; carefully remove the lid.
- Divide among individual bowls. Drizzle the lemon juice over each serving and enjoy!

Per serving: 335 Calories; 19.9g Fat; 6.2g Carbs; 33.4g Protein; 2.9g Sugars

58. The Perfect Tuna Salad

(Ready in about 10 minutes + chilling time | Servings 4)

INGREDIENTS

1 pound tuna, cut into bite-sized pieces
1 cup buckwheat
1/2 teaspoon dried or fresh dill
Salt and black pepper, to taste
2 cups water
1 white onion, thinly sliced
2 bell peppers, seeded and thinly sliced
1 carrot, grated
1 large-sized cucumber, thinly sliced
1/4 cup extra-virgin olive oil
2 tablespoons lemon juice, freshly squeezed

DIRECTIONS

- Place the tuna, buckwheat, dill, salt, black pepper, and water into your Cosori Pressure Cooker.
- Secure the lid. Choose the "Manual" setting, adjust to "Less/Low", and press "On/Start"; cook for 3 minutes.
- Once cooking is complete, use a quick pressure release; carefully remove the lid.
- Allow the fish and buckwheat to cool completely. Then, toss it with the remaining Ingredients and serve well chilled. Bon appétit!

Per serving: 238 Calories; 6.8g Fat; 14.1g Carbs; 30.1g Protein; 3.3g Sugars

59. Home-Style Spanish Paella

(Ready in about 15 minutes | Servings 6)

INGREDIENTS

3 teaspoons olive oil
1/2 ring of Chorizo sausage, sliced
1 onion, chopped
1 ½ cups basmati rice
2 cups water
1 cup tomato paste
1 red bell pepper, chopped
1 roasted yellow bell pepper, chopped
1 ½ pounds tiger shrimp, cleaned and divined

Sea salt, to taste
1/2 teaspoon ground black pepper
1/2 teaspoon sweet paprika
A pinch of saffron threads
1 bay leaf
1 cup frozen peas
1 cup frozen sweetcorn

DIRECTIONS

- Select the "Sauté/Brown" mode, adjust to "More/High", and press "On/Start". Heat the olive oil; now, brown the sausage and onion for 2 to 3 minutes.
- Add the rice and continue to cook an additional 3 minutes or until it starts to turn translucent.
- Stir the remaining Ingredients into your Cosori Pressure Cooker.
- Secure the lid. Choose the "Manual" mode and High pressure; cook for 6 minutes. Once cooking is complete, use a quick pressure release; carefully remove the lid. Serve warm.

Per serving: 335 Calories; 11.8g Fat; 35.8g Carbs; 31.6g Protein; 12.6g Sugars

60. Fresh Dill Shrimp Salad with Mayo

(Ready in about 10 minutes | Servings 4)

INGREDIENTS

1 pound shrimps, deveined and peeled
Fresh juice of 2 lemons
Salt and black pepper, to taste
1 red onion, chopped

1 stalk celery, chopped
1 tablespoon fresh dill, minced
1/2 cup mayonnaise
1 teaspoon Dijon mustard

DIRECTIONS

- Prepare your Cosori Pressure Cooker by adding 1 cup of water and a steamer basket to its bottom. Now, add the shrimps to the steamer basket.
- Top with lemon slices.
- Secure the lid. Choose the "Manual" mode and High pressure; cook for 2 minutes. Once cooking is complete, use a quick pressure release; carefully remove the lid.
- Add the remaining Ingredients and toss to combine well. Serve well chilled and enjoy!

Per serving: 220 Calories; 10.5g Fat; 7.3g Carbs; 25.4g Protein; 2.9g Sugars

VEGETABLES & SIDE DISHES

61. Braised Bok Choy with Kalamata Olives 76
62. Italian-Style Tomato Soup 77
63. Cabbage Soup with Cream, Celery and Ham 78
64. Creamy Broccoli and Potato Chowder 79
65. Double-Cheese Artichoke and Kale Dip 80
66. Vegetable Masala with Naan 81
67. Brussels Sprouts with Romano Cheese 82
68. Portobello Mushrooms with Tangy Tomato Sauce 83
69. Mediterranean Vegetable Kebabs 84
70. Piquant Chanterelle Mushrooms with Cabbage 85

61. Braised Bok Choy with Kalamata Olives

(Ready in about 10 minutes | Servings 4)

INGREDIENTS

1 pound Bok choy, leaves separated
2 teaspoons canola oil
3 tablespoons black sesame seeds
2 tablespoons soy sauce

1/2 teaspoon smoked paprika
Salt and ground black pepper, to taste
1/2 cup Kalamata olives, pitted and sliced

DIRECTIONS

- Prepare the Cosori Pressure Cooker by adding 1 ½ cups of water and a steamer basket to the bottom. Place the Bok choy in the steamer basket.
- Secure the lid. Choose the "Manual" mode and High pressure; cook for 4 minutes. Once cooking is complete, use a quick pressure release; carefully remove the lid.
- Transfer the Bok choy to a bowl and toss with the remaining Ingredients. Bon appétit!

Per serving: 178 Calories; 10.8g Fat; 14.3g Carbs; 12.8g Protein; 2.1g Sugars

62. Italian-Style Tomato Soup

(Ready in about 35 minutes | Servings 4)

INGREDIENTS

1 tablespoon olive oil
A bunch of scallions, chopped
1 garlic clove, minced
2 carrots, grated
1 celery, chopped
1 pounds tomatoes, seeded and chopped
4 cups roasted-vegetable broth
Sea salt, to taste
1/4 teaspoon freshly ground black pepper
1/2 teaspoon cayenne pepper
1/2 teaspoon dried basil
1/2 teaspoon dried oregano
1/2 cup double cream
1 tablespoon fresh Italian parsley, roughly chopped

DIRECTIONS

- Select the "Sauté/Brown" mode, adjust to "Normal/Medium", and press "On/Start". Now, heat the oil; sauté the scallions, garlic, carrot, and celery for approximately 5 minutes.
- Stir in the tomatoes, broth, salt, black pepper, cayenne pepper, basil, and oregano.
- Secure the lid. Choose the "Soup" mode, adjust to "Normal/Medium", and press "On/Start"; cook for 25 minutes.
- Once cooking is complete, use a quick pressure release; carefully remove the lid.
- Fold in the cream and purée the soup with an immersion blender. Serve topped with fresh parsley. Bon appétit!

Per serving: 175 Calories; 11.1g Fat; 12.5g Carbs; 7.7g Protein; 6.7g Sugars

63. Cabbage Soup with Cream, Celery and Ham

(Ready in about 30 minutes | Servings 4)

INGREDIENTS

1 ½ tablespoons olive oil
1 leek, chopped
1 celery rib, chopped
2 garlic cloves, chopped
1 pound cabbage, shredded
3 ½ cups broth, preferably homemade

Sea salt, to taste
1/2 teaspoon black peppercorns
2 bay leaves
1 cup fully cooked ham, cubed
1 cup double cream
1/4 cup fresh chives, chopped

DIRECTIONS

- Select the "Sauté/Brown" mode, adjust to "Normal/Medium", and press "On/Start"; add olive oil. Once hot, cook the leeks for 3 minutes or until they are softened.
- Stir in the celery and cook for 3 minutes more. Add a splash of broth if needed. Now, add the garlic and cook for 30 seconds more or until it is fragrant.
- Add the cabbage, broth, salt, black peppercorns, and bay leaves.
- Secure the lid. Choose the "Soup" mode, adjust to "Less/Low", and press "On/Start"; cook for 15 minutes.
- Once cooking is complete, use a quick pressure release; carefully remove the lid.
- Fold in the ham and double cream and continue to cook in the residual heat for 5 minutes longer.
- Taste, adjust the seasonings and serve in individual bowls, garnished with fresh chopped chives. Enjoy!

Per serving: 292 Calories; 19.5g Fat; 16.6g Carbs; 14.6g Protein; 7.9g Sugars

64. Creamy Broccoli and Potato Chowder

(Ready in about 30 minutes | Servings 6)

INGREDIENTS

1/2 cup leeks, chopped

1 pound broccoli, broken into small florets

1/2 pound celery, chopped

1 carrot, sliced

2 potatoes, peeled and diced

3 cups water

2 cups roasted-vegetable stock

Kosher salt, to taste

1/4 teaspoon ground black pepper

1/4 teaspoon red pepper flakes, crushed

1 cup sour cream

DIRECTIONS

- Simply place all of the above Ingredients, except for the sour cream, in your Cosori Pressure Cooker.
- Secure the lid. Choose the "Soup" mode, adjust to "Normal/Medium", and press "On/Start"; cook for 25 minutes.
- Once cooking is complete, use a quick pressure release; carefully remove the lid.
- Then, puree the soup with an immersion blender. Serve in individual bowls, garnished with a dollop of sour cream. Bon appétit!

Per serving: 193 Calories; 5.5g Fat; 28.6g Carbs; 9.2g Protein; 2.1g Sugars

65. Double-Cheese Artichoke and Kale Dip

(Ready in about 15 minutes | Servings 10)

INGREDIENTS

1 can (14-ounce) artichoke hearts, drained and roughly chopped
1/2 pound kale leaves, fresh or frozen torn into pieces
1 cup cream cheese
1 cup Colby cheese, shredded
1 cup mayonnaise
1 teaspoon yellow mustard
2 garlic cloves, minced
1 teaspoon shallot powder
1 teaspoon fennel seeds
Sea salt and ground black pepper, to taste

DIRECTIONS

- Place 1 cup of water and a metal rack in your Cosori Pressure Cooker.
- Then, thoroughly combine all the Ingredients in a casserole dish that is previously greased with a nonstick cooking spray; cover the casserole dish with a piece of aluminum foil, making a foil sling if needed.
- Lower the casserole dish onto the rack.
- Secure the lid. Choose the "Steam Vegetables" mode, adjust to "Normal/Medium", and press "On/Start"; cook for 7 minutes.
- Once cooking is complete, use a quick pressure release; carefully remove the lid.
- Serve with chips or pita wedges. Enjoy!

Per serving: 219 Calories; 19g Fat; 5.5g Carbs; 7.6g Protein; 1.7g Sugars

66. Vegetable Masala with Naan

(Ready in about 1 hour 20 minutes | Servings 6)

INGREDIENTS

1 tablespoon sesame oil
2 bell pepper, seeded and sliced
1 red chili pepper, seeded and sliced
1 teaspoon garlic paste
1/2 teaspoon fresh ginger, grated
1 tablespoon garam masala
1/2 teaspoon dhania
1/2 teaspoon haldi
1/2 teaspoon ground black pepper
Sea salt, to taste
1 cup water

Naan:
1 tablespoon dry active yeast
1 teaspoon sugar
2/3 cup warm water
2 ½ cups all-purpose flour
1/2 teaspoon salt
1/4 cup vegetable oil
1 egg

DIRECTIONS

- Select the "Sauté/Brown" mode, adjust to "Normal/Medium", and press "On/Start". Heat the oil until sizzling. Once hot, sauté the peppers, garlic, ginger, and spices. Add water and stir to combine.
- Secure the lid. Choose the "Manual" mode and High pressure; cook for 4 minutes. Once cooking is complete, use a quick pressure release; carefully remove the lid.
- Meanwhile, make the naan by mixing the yeast, sugar and 2 tablespoons of warm water; allow it sit for 5 to 6 minutes.
- Add the remaining Ingredients for naans; let it rest for about 1 hour at room temperature.
- Now, divide the dough into six balls; flatten the balls on a working surface.
- Heat up a large-sized pan over moderate heat. Cook the naans until they are golden on both sides. Serve these naans with the reserved vegetables and enjoy!

Per serving: 319 Calories; 12.7g Fat; 43.5g Carbs; 7.6g Protein; 1.7g Sugars

67. Brussels Sprouts with Romano Cheese

(Ready in about 15 minutes | Servings 4)

INGREDIENTS

1 ½ pounds Brussels sprouts, trimmed
3 tablespoons ghee
2 garlic cloves, minced
1/2 cup scallions, finely chopped
Salt, to taste

1/2 teaspoon freshly ground black pepper
1/2 teaspoon red pepper flakes
1 cup Romano cheese, grated

DIRECTIONS

- Place 1 cup of water and a steamer basket on the bottom of your Cosori Pressure Cooker. Place the Brussels sprouts in the steamer basket.
- Secure the lid. Choose the "Steam Vegetables" mode, adjust to "Normal/Medium", and press "On/Start"; cook for 7 minutes.
- Once cooking is complete, use a quick pressure release; carefully remove the lid.
- While the Brussels sprouts are still hot, add the ghee, garlic, scallions, salt, black pepper, red pepper, and Romano cheese; toss to coat well and serve.

Per serving: 261 Calories; 16.2g Fat; 20.1g Carbs; 13.2g Protein; 4.1g Sugars

68. Portobello Mushrooms with Tangy Tomato Sauce

(Ready in about 10 minutes | Servings 4)

INGREDIENTS

1 ½ pounds portobello mushrooms
1 cup vegetable stock
2 ripe tomatoes, chopped
2/3 teaspoon porcini powder
Sea salt and ground black pepper, to taste
2 garlic cloves, minced

1/2 teaspoon mustard seeds
1 teaspoon celery seeds
1 tablespoon apple cider vinegar
1 tablespoon dark soy sauce
1 tablespoon brown sugar
1/2 teaspoon liquid smoke

DIRECTIONS

- Add all of the above Ingredients to your Cosori Pressure Cooker; stir to combine well.
- Secure the lid. Choose the "Manual" mode and High pressure; cook for 4 minutes. Once cooking is complete, use a natural pressure release; carefully remove the lid.
- Serve immediately and enjoy!

Per serving: 89 Calories; 2.1g Fat; 14.2g Carbs; 6.2g Protein; 9.2g Sugars

69. Mediterranean Vegetable Kebabs

(Ready in about 10 minutes | Servings 4)

INGREDIENTS

1 head broccoli, broken into florets and blanched
2 bell peppers, seeded and diced
2 medium zucchinis, cut into 1-inch slices
8 ounces button mushrooms, whole
2 cups cherry tomatoes
4 tablespoons olive oil

Fresh juice of 1/2 lemon
Sea salt and ground black pepper, to taste
1 teaspoon dried oregano
1 teaspoon dried rosemary
1/4 teaspoon ground bay leaves
1/2 teaspoon crushed red pepper

DIRECTIONS

- Prepare your Cosori Pressure Cooker by adding 1 cup of water and a metal rack to its bottom.
- Thread the vegetables onto bamboo or wooden skewers.
- Drizzle them with olive oil and fresh lemon juice; add seasonings.
- Secure the lid. Choose the "Manual" mode and High pressure; cook for 3 minutes. Once cooking is complete, use a natural pressure release; carefully remove the lid. Bon appétit!

Per serving: 224 Calories; 14.3g Fat; 22.5g Carbs; 6.4g Protein; 13.4g Sugars

70. Piquant Chanterelle Mushrooms with Cabbage

(Ready in about 10 minutes | Servings 4)

INGREDIENTS

3 teaspoons olive oil
1/2 pound Chanterelle mushrooms, thinly sliced
1 pound purple cabbage, cut into wedges
2 red onions, cut into wedges
2 garlic cloves, smashed

1/3 cup Worcestershire sauce
2 tablespoons champagne vinegar
1 teaspoon cayenne pepper
Salt, to taste
1/2 teaspoon ground bay leaf
1/3 teaspoon white pepper
1/2 teaspoon adobo seasoning

DIRECTIONS

- Select the "Sauté/Brown" mode, adjust to "Normal/Medium", and press "On/Start"; heat the oil. Once hot, add the mushrooms; cook until they are lightly browned, about 4 minutes.
- Add the other Ingredients in the order listed above. Gently stir to combine.
- Secure the lid. Choose the "Manual" mode and High pressure; cook for 4 minutes. Once cooking is complete, use a quick pressure release; carefully remove the lid. Bon appétit!

Per serving: 121 Calories; 3.8g Fat; 20.3g Carbs; 4g Protein; 10.1g Sugars

VEGAN

71. Delicious Three-Pepper Chili 87
72. Classic Hummus Dip 88
73. Paprika Risotto with Tomatoes 89
74. Curry-Braised Cabbage with Root Vegetables 90
75. Zucchini with Tomato and Olives 91
76. Lentils with Kale and Cashew Cream 92
77. Baby Potatoes in Curry Sauce 93
78. Basmati Rice with Candy Onions and Peas 94
79. Fresh Lentil Salad with Peppers 95
80. Quinoa with Mushrooms and Herbs 96

71. Delicious Three-Pepper Chili

(Ready in about 20 minutes | Servings 6)

INGREDIENTS

2 tablespoons olive oil
1 red onion, chopped
3 cloves garlic minced or pressed
1 red bell pepper, diced
1 green bell pepper, diced
1 red chili pepper, minced
Sea salt and ground black pepper, to taste

1 teaspoon cayenne pepper
1/2 teaspoon ground cumin
2 cups vegetable stock
2 ripe tomatoes, chopped
2 (15-ounce) cans beans, drained and rinsed
1 handful fresh cilantro leaves, chopped
1/2 cup tortilla chips

DIRECTIONS

- Select the "Sauté/Brown" mode, adjust to "Normal/Medium", and press "On/Start". Now, heat the oil until sizzling.
- Sauté the onion tender and translucent. Add the garlic, peppers, salt, and pepper; continue to sauté until they are tender.
- Now, stir in the cayenne pepper, cumin, stock, tomatoes, and beans.
- Secure the lid. Choose the "Beans/Chili" mode, adjust to "Normal/Medium", and press "On/Start"; cook for 11 minutes.
- Once cooking is complete, use a quick pressure release; carefully remove the lid.
- Divide the chili between six serving bowls; top with fresh cilantro and tortilla chips. Enjoy!

Per serving: 204 Calories; 6.5g Fat; 27.9g Carbs; 10.4g Protein; 6.9g Sugars

72. Classic Hummus Dip

(Ready in about 35 minutes | Servings 8)

INGREDIENTS

10 cups water
3/4 pound dried chickpeas, soaked
2 tablespoons tahini
1/2 lemon, juiced
1 teaspoon granulated garlic

Salt and black pepper, to taste
1/3 teaspoon ground cumin
1/2 teaspoon cayenne pepper
1/2 teaspoon dried basil
3 tablespoon olive oil

DIRECTIONS

- Add water and the chickpeas to the Cosori Pressure Cooker.
- Secure the lid. Choose the "Beans/Chili" mode, adjust to "More/High", and press "On/Start"; cook for 30 minutes.
- Once cooking is complete, use a natural pressure release; carefully remove the lid.
- Now, drain your chickpeas, reserving the liquid. Transfer the chickpeas to a food processor. Add the tahini, lemon juice, and seasonings.
- Puree until it is creamy; gradually pour in the reserved liquid and olive oil until the mixture is smooth and uniform. Serve with a few sprinkles of cayenne pepper. Bon appétit!

Per serving: 186 Calories; 7.7g Fat; 22.8g Carbs; 7.6g Protein; 4g Sugars

73. Paprika Risotto with Tomatoes

(Ready in about 25 minutes | Servings 4)

INGREDIENTS

1 tablespoon sesame oil
1 yellow onion, peeled and chopped
2 cloves garlic, minced
1 cup tomatoes, pureed
1 carrot, chopped
1 tablespoon tomato powder
1 teaspoon curry powder

1 teaspoon citrus & ginger spice blend
1/2 teaspoon paprika
Sea salt and freshly ground black pepper, to taste
1 cup white rice, soaked for 30 minutes
2 ½ cups water

DIRECTIONS

- Select the "Sauté/Brown" mode, adjust to "Normal/Medium", and press "On/Start". Heat sesame oil until sizzling.
- Sweat the onion for 2 to 3 minutes. Add the garlic and cook an additional 30 to 40 seconds.
- Add the tomatoes and carrot; cook for a further 10 minutes, stirring periodically. Add the seasonings, rice, and water to the Cosori Pressure Cooker.
- Secure the lid. Choose the "Manual" setting, adjust to "Normal/Medium", and press "On/Start"; cook for 7 minutes.
- Once cooking is complete, use a quick pressure release; carefully remove the lid.
- Taste, adjust the seasonings and serve warm. Bon appétit!

Per serving: 251 Calories; 6.2g Fat; 44.1g Carbs; 4.2g Protein; 3g Sugars

74. Curry-Braised Cabbage with Root Vegetables

(Ready in about 20 minutes | Servings 4)

INGREDIENTS

2 tablespoons olive oil
1 medium-sized leek, chopped
2 cloves garlic, smashed
1 ½ pounds white cabbage, shredded
1 cup vegetable broth
1 cup tomatoes, puréed
1 parsnip, chopped
2 carrots, chopped
2 stalks celery, chopped
1 turnip, chopped

1/2 tablespoon fresh lime juice
1 teaspoon dried basil
1/2 teaspoon dried dill
1 teaspoon ground coriander
1 teaspoon ground turmeric
1 bay leaf
Kosher salt and ground black pepper, to taste
1 (14-ounce) can coconut milk

DIRECTIONS

- Select the "Sauté/Brown" mode, adjust to "Normal/Medium", and press "On/Start". Now, heat the oil and cook the leeks and garlic until tender and fragrant.
- After that, add the remaining Ingredients; stir to combine well.
- Secure the lid. Choose the "Soup" mode, adjust to "Less/Low", and press "On/Start"; cook for 15 minutes.
- Once cooking is complete, use a natural pressure release; carefully remove the lid.
- Ladle into soup bowls and serve immediately.

Per serving: 223 Calories; 8.2g Fat; 33.8g Carbs; 7.6g Protein; 15.1g Sugars

75. Zucchini with Tomato and Olives

(Ready in about 10 minutes | Servings 4)

INGREDIENTS

2 tablespoons garlic-infused olive oil
1 garlic clove, minced
1/2 cup scallions, chopped
1 pound zucchinis, sliced
1/2 cup tomato paste
1/2 cup vegetable broth
Salt, to taste

1/2 teaspoon ground black pepper
1/2 teaspoon dried oregano
1/2 teaspoon dried basil
1 teaspoon paprika
1/2 cup Kalamata olives, pitted and sliced

DIRECTIONS

- Select the "Sauté/Brown" mode, adjust to "Normal/Medium", and press "On/Start". Now, heat the oil; sauté the garlic and scallions for 2 minutes or until they are tender and fragrant.
- Add the zucchinis, tomato paste, broth, salt, black pepper, oregano, basil, and paprika.
- Secure the lid. Choose the "Steam Vegetables" mode, adjust to "Less/Low", and press "On/Start"; cook for 2 minutes.
- Once cooking is complete, use a quick pressure release; carefully remove the lid.
- Serve garnished with Kalamata olives. Bon appétit!

Per serving: 143 Calories; 9.4g Fat; 12.7g Carbs; 5.6g Protein; 4.4g Sugars

76. Lentils with Kale and Cashew Cream

(Ready in about 15 minutes | Servings 4)

INGREDIENTS

2 teaspoons toasted sesame oil
1 yellow onion, chopped
2 cloves garlic, pressed
1 teaspoon fresh ginger, grated
1 bell pepper, chopped
1 serrano pepper, chopped
1/2 teaspoon ground allspice
1/2 teaspoon ground cumin
1/2 teaspoon dried basil

1 teaspoon dried parsley flakes
Sea salt and black pepper, to taste
1 ½ cups tomato purée
2 cups vegetable stock
1 cup beluga lentils
2 cups kale leaves, torn into pieces
1 teaspoon fresh lemon juice
1/2 cup cashew cream

DIRECTIONS

- Select the "Sauté/Brown" mode, adjust to "Normal/Medium", and press "On/Start". Now, heat the oil; sauté the onion until tender and translucent.
- Then, add the garlic, ginger, and peppers; continue to sauté until they have softened.
- Add the seasonings, tomato purée, stock, and lentils.
- Secure the lid. Choose the "Beans/Chili" mode, adjust to "Normal/Medium", and press "On/Start"; cook for 11 minutes.
- Once cooking is complete, use a natural pressure release; carefully remove the lid.
- Add the kale and lemon juice; seal the lid again and let it sit until thoroughly warmed. Serve dolloped with cashew cream. Enjoy!

Per serving: 311 Calories; 22.9g Fat; 21.8g Carbs; 9.9g Protein; 6.7g Sugars

77. Baby Potatoes in Curry Sauce

(Ready in about 15 minutes | Servings 6)

INGREDIENTS

1 tablespoon canola oil
1/2 cup scallions, chopped
2 cloves garlic, minced
1 teaspoon red chili pepper, minced
2 pounds baby potatoes, diced
1 tablespoon curry paste
1 cup water

1 cup vegetable broth
1 cup full-fat coconut milk
Salt, to taste
1/2 teaspoon ground black pepper
1 teaspoon cayenne pepper
1 teaspoon cumin

DIRECTIONS

- Select the "Sauté/Brown" mode, adjust to "Normal/Medium", and press "On/Start". Now, heat the canola oil until sizzling; sauté the scallions until just tender.
- Add the garlic and chili pepper; allow it to cook an additional 30 seconds, stirring continuously. Add the remaining Ingredients.
- Secure the lid. Choose the "Steam Potatoes" mode, adjust to "Less/Low", and press "On/Start"; cook for 10 minutes.
- Once cooking is complete, use a quick pressure release; carefully remove the lid. Serve hot.

Per serving: 246 Calories; 12.4g Fat; 31.1g Carbs; 5.3g Protein; 3.1g Sugars

78. Basmati Rice with Candy Onions and Peas

(Ready in about 15 minutes | Servings 3)

INGREDIENTS

1 cup basmati rice, rinsed
1 ¼ cups water
Kosher salt and white pepper, to taste
2 tablespoons fresh coriander
4 ounces fresh green peas
2 fresh green chilies, chopped

1 garlic clove, pressed
1/2 cup candy onions, chopped
4 whole cloves
1/2 cup creamed coconut
1 tablespoon fresh lime juice

DIRECTIONS

- Combine all of the above Ingredients, except for the lime juice, in your Cosori Pressure Cooker.
- Secure the lid. Choose the "White Rice" mode, adjust to "Normal/Medium", and press "On/Start"; cook for 6 minutes.
- Once cooking is complete, use a natural pressure release; carefully remove the lid.
- Serve in individual bowls, drizzled with fresh lime juice. Bon appétit!

Per serving: 306 Calories; 16.7g Fat; 42.7g Carbs; 9.1g Protein; 18.2g Sugars

79. Fresh Lentil Salad with Peppers

(Ready in about 20 minutes | Servings 4)

INGREDIENTS

3 cups water

1 ½ cups dried French green lentils, rinsed

2 bay leaves

A bunch of spring onions, roughly chopped

2 garlic cloves, minced

2 carrots, shredded

1 green bell pepper, thinly sliced

1 red bell pepper, thinly sliced

1/2 cup radishes, thinly sliced

1 cucumber, thinly sliced

1/4 cup extra-virgin olive oil

2 tablespoons balsamic vinegar

1/4 cup fresh basil, snipped

1 teaspoon mixed peppercorns, freshly cracked

Sea salt, to taste

DIRECTIONS

- Place the water, lentils, and bay leaves in your Cosori Pressure Cooker.
- Secure the lid. Choose the "Beans/Chili" mode, adjust to "Normal/Medium", and press "On/Start"; cook for 11 minutes.
- Once cooking is complete, use a quick pressure release; carefully remove the lid.
- Drain the green lentils and discard the bay leaves; transfer to a large salad bowl.
- Add the spring onions, garlic, carrots, bell peppers, radishes, cucumber, olive oil, vinegar, and basil. Season with crushed peppercorns and sea salt.
- Toss to combine and place in your refrigerator until ready to serve. Bon appétit!

Per serving: 183 Calories; 13.8g Fat; 13.7g Carbs; 3.5g Protein; 4g Sugars

80. Quinoa with Mushrooms and Herbs

(Ready in about 10 minutes | Servings 4)

INGREDIENTS

2 cups dry quinoa
3 cups water
2 tablespoons olive oil
1 onion, chopped
1 bell pepper, chopped
2 garlic cloves, chopped
2 cups Cremini mushrooms, thinly sliced
1/2 teaspoon sea salt
1/3 teaspoon ground black pepper, or more to taste
1 teaspoon cayenne pepper
1/2 teaspoon dried dill
1/4 teaspoon ground bay leaf

DIRECTIONS

- Add the quinoa and water to the Cosori Pressure Cooker.
- Secure the lid. Choose the "Manual" setting, adjust to "Normal/Medium", and press "On/Start"; cook for 1 minutes.
- Once cooking is complete, use a natural pressure release; carefully remove the lid.
- Drain the quinoa and set it aside.
- Select the "Sauté/Brown" mode, adjust to "Normal/Medium", and press "On/Start". Once hot, heat the oil. Then, sauté the onion until tender and translucent.
- Add the bell pepper, garlic, and mushrooms and continue to sauté for 1 to 2 minutes more or until they are fragrant. Stir the remaining Ingredients into the Cosori Pressure Cooker.
- Add the reserved quinoa and stir to combine well. Serve warm. Bon appétit!

Per serving: 401 Calories; 12.1g Fat; 60.2g Carbs; 14.1g Protein; 2.7g Sugars

SNACKS & APPETIZERS

81. Spicy Paprika Mushrooms	98
82. Carrot Sticks in Wine-Butter Sauce	99
83. Summer BBQ Chicken Wings	100
84. Easy Spicy Ribs	101
85. BBQ Cheese and Chicken Dip	102
86. Cheesy Cauliflower Balls	103
87. Three-Cheese Italian Dip	104
88. Baba Ganoush with a Twist	105
89. Deviled Eggs with Chives and Mayo	106
90. Barbecued Little Wieners	107

81. Spicy Paprika Mushrooms

(Ready in about 10 minutes | Servings 5)

INGREDIENTS

20 ounces fresh white mushrooms
1 cup water
1 tablespoon apple cider vinegar
3 tablespoons soy sauce
1 tablespoon peanut butter
1 tablespoon molasses

2 garlic cloves, minced
2 tablespoons olive oil
1/2 teaspoon hot sauce
Sea salt and ground black pepper, to taste
1 teaspoon paprika

DIRECTIONS

- Add all Ingredients to your Cosori Pressure Cooker.
- Secure the lid. Choose the "Manual" setting, adjust to "Normal/Medium", and press "On/Start"; cook for 5 minutes.
- Once cooking is complete, use a quick pressure release; carefully remove the lid; remove the mushrooms from the cooking liquid.
- Select the "Sauté/Brown" mode, adjust to "Less/Low", and press "On/Start". Continue to simmer until the sauce has reduced and thickened.
- Place the reserved mushrooms in a serving bowl, add the sauce and serve.

Per serving: 124 Calories; 8.1g Fat; 10.2g Carbs; 4.4g Protein; 7.7g Sugars

82. Carrot Sticks in Wine-Butter Sauce

(Ready in about 10 minutes | Servings 4)

INGREDIENTS

1 pound carrots, cut into sticks
1/2 cup dry white wine
1/2 cup water
Sea salt and white pepper, to taste
1/2 stick butter, softened

2 tablespoons agave nectar
1 teaspoon ground allspice
1/2 teaspoon caraway seeds
1 tablespoon fresh lime juice

DIRECTIONS

- Add all of the above Ingredients to the Cosori Pressure Cooker.
- Secure the lid. Choose the "Steam Vegetables" setting, adjust to "Less/Low", and press "On/Start"; cook for 2 minutes.
- Once cooking is complete, use a quick pressure release; carefully remove the lid
- Transfer to a serving bowl and enjoy!

Per serving: 199 Calories; 14.9g Fat; 13.7g Carbs; 4.5g Protein; 6.2g Sugars

83. Summer BBQ Chicken Wings

(Ready in about 20 minutes | Servings 3)

INGREDIENTS

1 cup water
6 chicken wings

For the Barbecue Sauce:
1/3 cup water
1/3 cup ketchup
2 tablespoons brown sugar
2 tablespoons blackstrap molasses
1 tablespoon mustard

1 tablespoon cider vinegar
1 tablespoon olive oil
1 teaspoon garlic, minced
1 teaspoon chipotle powder
1/4 teaspoon sea salt
1/4 teaspoon freshly ground black pepper
1/4 teaspoon ground allspice

DIRECTIONS

- Pour 1 cup of water into the base of your Cosori Pressure Cooker.
- Now, arrange the wings on a steaming basket. Transfer the steaming basket to the Cosori Pressure Cooker.
- Secure the lid. Choose the "Poultry" setting, adjust to "Normal/Medium", and press "On/Start"; cook for 15 minutes.
- Once cooking is complete, use a quick pressure release; carefully remove the lid.
- In a pan, combine all of the Ingredients for the sauce and bring to a boil. Remove from the heat and stir well. Add the chicken wings and serve. Bon appétit!

Per serving: 204 Calories; 6.7g Fat; 23.1g Carbs; 13.2g Protein; 20.1g Sugars

84. Easy Spicy Ribs

(Ready in about 30 minutes | Servings 6)

INGREDIENTS

1 ½ pounds baby back ribs
1 teaspoon salt
1/2 teaspoon ground black pepper
1 teaspoon smoked paprika
1/2 teaspoon ancho chili powder
1/2 teaspoon granulated garlic
1 teaspoon shallot powder
1/2 teaspoon mustard seeds

1 teaspoon celery seeds
1/2 cup whiskey
1 cup ketchup
1/3 cup dark brown sugar
1/4 cup rice vinegar
1 teaspoon fish sauce
1 teaspoon Worcestershire sauce

DIRECTIONS

- Season the ribs with salt, black pepper, paprika, chili powder, garlic, shallot powder, mustard seeds, and celery seeds.
- Add the seasoned ribs to the Cosori Pressure Cooker.
- In a mixing bowl, thoroughly combine the whiskey, ketchup, sugar, vinegar, fish sauce, and Worcestershire sauce.
- Then, pour the sauce into the Cosori Pressure Cooker.
- Secure the lid. Choose the "Meat/Stew" setting, adjust to "Less/Low", and press "On/Start"; cook for 25 minutes.
- Once cooking is complete, use a natural pressure release; carefully remove the lid. Reserve the ribs.
- Select the "Sauté/Brown" mode, adjust to "Less/Low", and press "On/Start". Simmer the sauce until it has reduced to your desired thickness. Pour the glaze over the ribs and serve. Bon appétit!

Per serving: 359 Calories; 17.9g Fat; 28g Carbs; 22.8g Protein; 25.1g Sugars

85. BBQ Cheese and Chicken Dip

(Ready in about 10 minutes | Servings 12)

INGREDIENTS

1 pound chicken white meat, boneless
1 cup barbecue sauce
1/3 cup water
6 ounces Ricotta cheese
3 ounces blue cheese dressing
1 parsnip, chopped

1/2 teaspoon dried rosemary
1/2 teaspoon cayenne pepper
1/4 teaspoon ground black pepper, or more to taste
Sea salt, to taste

DIRECTIONS

- Place all of the above Ingredients in your Cosori Pressure Cooker.
- Secure the lid. Choose the "Manual" setting, adjust to "Less/Low", and press "On/Start"; cook for 6 minutes.
- Once cooking is complete, use a natural pressure release; carefully remove the lid.
- Transfer to a serving bowl and serve warm or at room temperature. Bon appétit!

Per serving: 179 Calories; 7.5g Fat; 14.3g Carbs; 12.9g Protein; 10.3g Sugars

86. Cheesy Cauliflower Balls

(Ready in about 20 minutes | Servings 6)

INGREDIENTS

1 pound cauliflower, broken into small florets
2 tablespoons butter
2 cloves garlic, minced
1/2 cup Parmesan cheese, grated
2 eggs, beaten

1 cup Swiss cheese, shredded
2 tablespoons fresh parsley, minced
1 teaspoon cayenne pepper
Sea salt and ground black pepper, to taste

DIRECTIONS

- Prepare your Cosori Pressure Cooker by adding 1 cup of water and a steamer basket to its bottom.
- Place the cauliflower florets in the steamer basket.
- Secure the lid. Choose the "Steam Vegetables" setting, adjust to "Less/Low", and press "On/Start"; cook for 2 minutes.
- Once cooking is complete, use a quick pressure release; carefully remove the lid.
- Transfer the cauliflower florets to your blender. Add the remaining Ingredients; process until everything is well incorporated.
- Roll the cauliflower mixture into bite-sized balls. Bake in the preheated oven at 400 degrees F for 16 minutes. Bon appétit!

Per serving: 194 Calories; 13.8g Fat; 6.5g Carbs; 11.6g Protein; 1.8g Sugars

87. Three-Cheese Italian Dip

(Ready in about 10 minutes | Servings 10)

INGREDIENTS

8 ounces Asiago cheese, grated
9 ounces Mozzarella cheese, crumbled
2 ripe Roma tomatoes, puréed
8 ounces pancetta, chopped
1/2 cup green olives, pitted and halved
1 bell pepper, chopped
1 teaspoon garlic powder
1 teaspoon shallot powder
1 teaspoon porcini powder
1 teaspoon dried oregano
1 teaspoon dried basil
1 teaspoon dried marjoram
2/3 cup beef bone broth
6 ounces Parmigiano-Reggiano cheese, grated

DIRECTIONS

- Combine all Ingredients, except for the Parmigiano-Reggiano cheese, in your Cosori Pressure Cooker.
- Secure the lid. Choose the "Manual" setting, adjust to "Less/Low", and press "On/Start"; cook for 5 minutes.
- Once cooking is complete, use a natural pressure release; carefully remove the lid.
- Top with Parmigiano-Reggiano cheese; cover and allow it to sit in the residual heat until the cheese is melted. Bon appétit!

Per serving: 209 Calories; 11.4g Fat; 5.3g Carbs; 21.1g Protein; 3.3g Sugars

88. Baba Ganoush with a Twist

(Ready in about 10 minutes | Servings 10)

INGREDIENTS

1 cup water
3/4 pound eggplant
3 tablespoons olive oil
1/2 cup yellow onion, chopped
1 garlic cloves, roasted and 1 raw, crushed
Sea salt, to taste
1 teaspoon fresh oregano, chopped
1/3 teaspoon cayenne pepper
1/4 teaspoon ground black pepper, or more to taste
1 tablespoon fresh lime juice
1/4 cup tahini, plus more as needed
1/4 cup brine-cured black olives, brine-cured

DIRECTIONS

- Add water and a steaming basket to the base of your Cosori Pressure Cooker. Place the eggplant in the steaming basket.
- Secure the lid. Choose the "Manual" setting, adjust to "Less/Low", and press "On/Start"; cook for 4 minutes.
- Once cooking is complete, use a quick pressure release; carefully remove the lid.
- Drain the excess water out of the eggplant. Then, peel and slice the eggplant.
- Select the "Sauté/Brown" mode, adjust to "Normal/Medium", and press "On/Start"; add the oil. Once hot, cook the eggplant with the onions and garlic until they have softened.
- Season with salt, oregano, cayenne pepper, and ground black pepper. Transfer the mixture to your blender or food processor.
- Add the lime juice, tahini, and olives. Blend until everything is well incorporated. Serve well chilled and enjoy!

Per serving: 209 Calories; 18.9g Fat; 8.5g Carbs; 4.6g Protein; 1.5g Sugars

89. Deviled Eggs with Chives and Mayo

(Ready in about 20 minutes | Servings 8)

INGREDIENTS

1 ½ cups water
8 eggs
3 teaspoons mayonnaise
1 tablespoon sour cream
1 teaspoon gourmet mustard

1/2 teaspoon hot sauce
1/3 teaspoon ground black pepper
Crunchy sea salt, to taste
3 tablespoons fresh chives, thinly sliced

DIRECTIONS

- Add the water and a steaming basket to the base of your Cosori Pressure Cooker.
- Now, arrange the eggs in the steaming basket. Transfer the steaming basket to the Cosori Pressure Cooker.
- Secure the lid. Choose the "Manual" setting, adjust to "Less/Low", and press "On/Start"; cook for 13 minutes.
- Once cooking is complete, use a quick pressure release; carefully remove the lid.
- Peel the eggs under running water. Remove the yolks and smash them with a fork; reserve.
- Now, mix the mayonnaise, sour cream, gourmet mustard, hot sauce, black pepper, and salt; add reserved yolks and mash everything.
- Fill the whites with this mixture, heaping it lightly. Garnish with fresh chives and place in the refrigerator until ready to serve. Bon appétit!

Per serving: 138 Calories; 10.4g Fat; 1.2g Carbs; 9.1g Protein; 0.7g Sugars

90. Barbecued Little Wieners

(Ready in about 10 minutes | Servings 12)

INGREDIENTS

2 (16-ounce) packages little wieners
1/2 (18-ounce) bottle barbeque sauce
1/2 cup ketchup
3 tablespoons honey
1/2 yellow onion, chopped

2 jalapenos, sliced
1 teaspoon garlic powder
1 teaspoon cumin powder
1/2 teaspoon mustard powder

DIRECTIONS

- Add the little wieners, barbecue sauce, ketchup, honey, onion, jalapenos, garlic powder, cumin, and the mustard powder to the Cosori Pressure Cooker. Stir to combine well.
- Secure the lid. Choose the "Steam Vegetables" setting, adjust to "Less/Low", and press "On/Start"; cook for 2 minutes.
- Once cooking is complete, use a natural pressure release; carefully remove the lid.
- You can thicken the sauce to your desired thickness on the "Sauté" function. Serve warm with toothpicks. Bon appétit!

Per serving: 333 Calories; 23.4g Fat; 19.6g Carbs; 10g Protein; 13.2g Sugars

DESSERTS

91. Butterscotch Mini Lava Cakes 109
92. Grandma's Summer Compote 110
93. Cardamom Millet Pudding with Dates 111
94. Coconut Cherry Cobbler 112
95. Chocolate Cheesecake with Coconut and Raisins 113
96. Fall Maple Crumble Pie 114
97. Lemon Pots de Crème 115
98. Rice Pudding with Dates 116
99. Chocolate Dream Dessert with Almonds 117
100. Grandma's Festive Cake with Walnuts 118

91. Butterscotch Mini Lava Cakes

(Ready in about 30 minutes | Servings 6)

INGREDIENTS

1 stick butter
6 ounces butterscotch morsels
3/4 cup powdered sugar
3 eggs, whisked

1/2 teaspoon vanilla extract
7 tablespoons all-purpose flour
A pinch of coarse salt

DIRECTIONS

- Add 1 ½ cups of water and a metal rack to the Cosori Pressure Cooker. Line a standard-size muffin tin with muffin papers.
- In a microwave-safe bowl, microwave the butter and butterscotch morsels for about 40 seconds. Stir in the powdered sugar.
- Add the remaining Ingredients. Spoon the batter into the prepared muffin tin.
- Secure the lid. Choose the "Bake" setting, adjust to "Less/Low", and press "On/Start"; cook for 20 minutes.
- Once cooking is complete, use a quick pressure release; carefully remove the lid.
- To remove, let it cool for 5 to 6 minutes. Run a small knife around the sides of each cake and serve. Enjoy!

Per serving: 393 Calories; 21.1g Fat; 45.6g Carbs; 5.6g Protein; 35.4g Sugars

92. Grandma's Summer Compote

(Ready in about 20 minutes | Servings 5)

INGREDIENTS

1/2 pound peaches, pitted and halved
1/2 pound pears, cored and quartered
1 cup prunes, pitted
1/4 cup granulated sugar
1 tablespoon fresh apple juice
1 tablespoon fresh lemon juice

1/2 teaspoon apple pie spice mix
1 cinnamon stick
1 teaspoon whole cloves
1 large vanilla bean pod, split open lengthwise
2 cups water

DIRECTIONS

- Add all of the above Ingredients to your Cosori Pressure Cooker.
- Secure the lid. Choose the "Manual" setting, adjust to "Less/Low", and press "On/Start"; cook for 5 minutes.
- Once cooking is complete, use a natural pressure release for 10 minutes; carefully remove the lid.
- Serve warm or at room temperature. Enjoy!

Per serving: 164 Calories; 0.3g Fat; 42.9g Carbs; 1.4g Protein; 16.9g Sugars

93. Cardamom Millet Pudding with Dates

(Ready in about 15 minutes | Servings 4)

INGREDIENTS

1 ½ cups millet
1 ½ cups water
1 (14-ounce) can coconut milk

1/2 cup Medjool dates, finely chopped
1/2 teaspoon ground cardamom
1/2 teaspoon ground cinnamon

DIRECTIONS

- Add all of the above Ingredients to your Cosori Pressure Cooker; stir to combine well.
- Secure the lid. Choose the "Manual" setting, adjust to "Less/Low", and press "On/Start"; cook for 1 minute.
- Once cooking is complete, use a natural pressure release for 10 minutes; carefully remove the lid.
- Serve warm or at room temperature.

Per serving: 320 Calories; 3.3g Fat; 63.1g Carbs; 9.3g Protein; 6.7g Sugars

94. Coconut Cherry Cobbler

(Ready in about 25 minutes | Servings 6)

INGREDIENTS

30 ounces cherry pie filling
1 box yellow cake mix
1/2 cup coconut butter, melted
1/2 teaspoon ground cinnamon
1/2 teaspoon ground cardamom
1/4 teaspoon grated nutmeg

DIRECTIONS

- Add 1 cup of water and metal rack to the Cosori Pressure Cooker. Place the cherry pie filling in a pan.
- Mix the remaining Ingredients; spread the batter over the cherry pie filling evenly.
- Secure the lid. Choose the "Manual" setting, adjust to "Normal/Medium", and press "On/Start"; cook for 10 minutes.
- Once cooking is complete, use a natural pressure release for 10 minutes; carefully remove the lid.
- Serve with whipped topping. Enjoy!

Per serving: 499 Calories; 16.2g Fat; 82g Carbs; 4.5g Protein; 24.3g Sugars

95. Chocolate Cheesecake with Coconut and Raisins

(Ready in about 40 minutes | Servings 8)

INGREDIENTS

10 ounces cream cheese
7 ounces sour cheese
1 cup granulated sugar
3 eggs
2 tablespoons cornstarch
1 teaspoon vanilla extract
14 ounces chocolate cookies, crumbled

1/3 cup raisins, soaked for 15 minutes
3 teaspoons coconut oil

Topping:
4 ounces dark chocolate, melted
1 cup sweetened coconut milk
1/2 cup coconut, shredded

DIRECTIONS

- In a mixing bowl, thoroughly combine the cream cheese, sour cream, and sugar. Add the eggs and mix again; add the cornstarch and vanilla.
- In another bowl, thoroughly combine the cookies, raisins, and coconut oil. Press the crust into the bottom of a cake pan.
- Spread the cheesecake mixture over the crust.
- Add 1 ½ cups of water and metal trivet to the Cosori Pressure Cooker. Lower the pan onto the trivet. Cover with a foil, making a foil sling.
- Secure the lid. Choose the "Bake" setting, adjust to "More/High", and press "On/Start"; cook for 30 minutes.
- Once cooking is complete, use a quick pressure release; carefully remove the lid.
- Meanwhile, make the topping by vigorously whisking all the Ingredients. Spread the topping over the cake.
- Place in your refrigerator to cool completely. Enjoy!

Per serving: 575 Calories; 35.6g Fat; 54.1g Carbs; 11.1g Protein; 33.1g Sugars

96. Fall Maple Crumble Pie

(Ready in about 25 minutes | Servings 6)

INGREDIENTS

2 pears, cored, peeled and sliced
10 plums, pitted and halved
3/4 cup rolled oats
3 tablespoons flour
1/4 cup sugar
2 tablespoons maple syrup

2 tablespoons caramel syrup, plus more for topping
2 tablespoons fresh orange juice
1 teaspoon ground cinnamon
A pinch of salt
3 tablespoons coconut oil

DIRECTIONS

- Arrange the pears and plums in the bottom of a lightly buttered baking pan.
- In a mixing bowl, thoroughly combine the rolled oats, flour, sugar, maple syrup, caramel syrup, orange juice, cinnamon, salt and the coconut oil.
- Top the prepared pears and plums with the oat layer. Now, distribute the oat layer evenly using a spatula.
- Add 1 cup of water and a metal trivet to your Cosori Pressure Cooker. Lower the baking pan onto the trivet. Cover with a sheet of foil.
- Secure the lid. Choose the "Manual" setting, adjust to "Normal/Medium", and press "On/Start"; cook for 10 minutes.
- Once cooking is complete, use a natural pressure release for 10 minutes; carefully remove the lid.
- Remove the foil and let the crumble cool to room temperature before serving. Bon appétit!

Per serving: 227 Calories; 8.1g Fat; 42.8g Carbs; 3.4g Protein; 28.1g Sugars

97. Lemon Pots de Crème

(Ready in about 30 minutes | Servings 4)

INGREDIENTS

1 stick butter, softened
1 ¼ cups sugar
3 eggs
1 large egg yolks
1/2 cup fresh lemon juice
1 tablespoon lemon zest, finely grated

A pinch of salt
2 teaspoons cornstarch
1/4 cup heavy whipping cream
6 tablespoons blueberries
Mint leaves, for garnish

DIRECTIONS

- Beat the butter and sugar with an electric mixer. Gradually, add the eggs and yolks; mix until pale and smooth.
- Add the lemon juice and lemon zest; add the salt and cornstarch; mix to combine well. Pour the mixture into four jars; cover your jars with the lids.
- Add 1 cup of water and a trivet to the Cosori Pressure Cooker. Lower the jars onto the trivet;
- Secure the lid. Choose the "Manual" setting, adjust to "Normal/Medium", and press "On/Start"; cook for 15 minutes.
- Once cooking is complete, use a natural pressure release for 10 minutes; carefully remove the lid.
- Serve well-chilled, garnished with heavy whipping cream, blueberries, and mint leaves. Bon appétit!

Per serving: 445 Calories; 30.1g Fat; 40.6g Carbs; 5.4g Protein; 36.7g Sugars

98. Rice Pudding with Dates

(Ready in about 15 minutes | Servings 3)

INGREDIENTS

2 teaspoons coconut oil, softened
1 ½ cups jasmine rice, rinsed
1 ½ cups water
10 dates, pitted, soaked and chopped

2 eggs, beaten
1 teaspoon pure vanilla extract
1/8 teaspoon pumpkin pie spice

DIRECTIONS

- Select the "Sauté/Brown" mode, adjust to "Normal/Medium", and press "On/Start". Now, add the coconut oil and rice; stir until it is well coated.
- Add the remaining Ingredients and stir again.
- Secure the lid. Choose the "White Rice" setting, adjust to "Less/Low", and press "On/Start"; cook for 3 minutes.
- Once cooking is complete, use a natural pressure release for 10 minutes; carefully remove the lid.
- Divide between three dessert bowls and serve with double cream. Enjoy!

Per serving: 270 Calories; 12.5g Fat; 41.1g Carbs; 6g Protein; 14.2g Sugars

99. Chocolate Dream Dessert with Almonds

(Ready in about 15 minutes | Servings 3)

INGREDIENTS

3 eggs
2 tablespoons butter
3 tablespoons whole milk
3 tablespoons honey
1 teaspoon pure vanilla extract

1/4 teaspoon freshly grated nutmeg
1/4 teaspoon ground cardamom
A pinch of salt
1 cup almond flour
3 chocolate cookies, chunks

DIRECTIONS

- In a mixing bowl, beat the eggs with butter. Now, add the milk and continue mixing until well combined.
- Add the remaining Ingredients in the order listed above. Divide the batter among 3 ramekins.
- Add 1 cup of water and a metal trivet to the Cosori Pressure Cooker. Cover the ramekins with foil and lower them onto the trivet.
- Secure the lid. Choose the "Manual" setting, adjust to "Normal/Medium", and press "On/Start"; cook for 12 minutes.
- Once cooking is complete, use a quick pressure release; carefully remove the lid.
- Transfer the ramekins to a wire rack and allow them to cool slightly before serving. Enjoy!

Per serving: 304 Calories; 18.9g Fat; 23.8g Carbs; 10g Protein; 21.1g Sugars

100. Grandma's Festive Cake with Walnuts

(Ready in about 45 minutes | Servings 6)

INGREDIENTS

1 ¼ cups coconut flour
1/4 cup walnuts, ground
1 ½ teaspoons baking powder
1 cup sugar
1 teaspoon ground cinnamon
1/2 teaspoon grated nutmeg

1 teaspoon orange zest, finely grated
1/4 teaspoon ground star anise
2 eggs plus 1 egg yolk, whisked
1/2 stick butter, at room temperature
3/4 cup double cream

DIRECTIONS

- Add 1 ½ cups of water and a steamer rack to your Cosori Pressure Cooker. Spritz the inside of a baking pan with a nonstick cooking spray.
- Thoroughly combine the dry Ingredients. Then, mix the wet Ingredients. Add the wet mixture to the dry flour mixture and mix until everything is well incorporated.
- Scrape the batter mixture into the prepared baking pan. Now, cover the baking pan with a piece of foil, making a foil sling.
- Place the baking pan on the steamer rack.
- Secure the lid. Choose the "Bake" setting, adjust to "More/High", and press "On/Start"; cook for 30 minutes.
- Once cooking is complete, use a natural pressure release for 10 minutes; carefully remove the lid.
- Just before serving, dust the top of the cake with icing sugar. Lastly cut the cake into wedges and serve. Bon appétit!

Per serving: 244 Calories; 17.3g Fat; 21.3g Carbs; 2.7g Protein; 18.8g Sugars

Made in the USA
Columbia, SC
29 November 2019